D1395616

Mother's Ruin

John Watney

MOTHER'S RUIN

A History of Gin

PETER OWEN · LONDON

ISBN 0 7206 0234 3

PETER OWEN LIMITED
20 Holland Park Avenue London W11 3QU

First British Commonwealth edition 1976
© John Watney 1976

Printed in Great Britain by
Villiers Publications Ltd London NW5

CONTENTS

Illustrations

Illustrations are reproduced by courtesy of the following: Mr Roger Musgrave (2); the Trustees of the British Museum (4); Buchanan Booth's Agencies Ltd (5, 12); W. & A. Gilbey Ltd (6, 7, 10 11); The Salvation Army (8, 9).

I

Geneva

Gin is the youngest of the classic alcoholic drinks. Beer was brewed in Egypt five thousand years ago; the Ancient Greeks knew how to make wine; a form of whisky, called usquebaugh, was probably being distilled in the shaded and secret glens beyond Hadrian's Wall and the Roman reach sixteen hundred years ago; gin, however, goes back little more than four hundred years.

It originated in Holland, where distillers had for some time been using rye as a basis for making a form of *eau de vie*. It had a flat unpleasant taste, and as it was mainly used as a medicine, the local apothecaries began to flavour it, to make it more palatable. Various ingredients were tested, but it was soon found that the best agent was the juice of the juniper berry.

The juniper, a small coniferous evergreen, grew in profusion. Its bluish-black berries added an attractive bitterness to the medicine and completely disguised the original taste. In addition, the oil from the juniper berry had a considerable medicinal value of its own. This 'double' medicine was reputed to cure a number of internal complaints, particularly those connected with over-acidity of the stomach, such as dyspepsia. Apart from helping the digestive system generally, it was also supposed to cure gout as it counteracted the effect of heavy red wine, and it alleviated the pain from gall-stones.

The Father of Gin, if such a title is applicable to any one man, was the Dutch chemist, Professor Sylvius of Leyden Uni-

9

versity, who, in the middle of the sixteenth century, reputedly produced such a pure form of the medicine that it came to be in tremendous demand throughout northern Europe. Leyden became known as the source of the best kind of therapeutic medicine.

It was not, however, until the following century, when Holland became the main battlefield for various warring countries, that gin began to take on a wider significance. When the armies of France invaded the Netherlands, the troops, in the absence of their own drinks, took to the strongly-flavoured local alcohol. They learned the method of making it and, as the French for juniper is *genièvre,* called it *eau de genièvre.*

When English soldiers, under the leadership of Sir Sidney Smith, trudged wearily across the low-lying Dutch polders, they too came across this warming and invigorating drink. On asking what it was called, they were told *eau de genièvre.* This was altogether too much of a mouthful for the English, so they shortened it, first to *genever* or *geneva,* and then to *gin.*

When the soldiers returned home they brought back with them memories of the excellent genever that had sustained them during the hard, cold campaigns in the Low Countries. All who had tried it agreed that it had the extraordinary power of endowing the faint-hearted or dispirited with an artificial courage and verve. Soon people were talking of the 'Dutch courage' invariably shown by those who drank genever.

In the England of the Thirty Years War the most popular drinks were ale and beer, with the wealthy drinking wine. Brandy, which could be obtained cheaply from France, was the favourite distilled drink, being infinitely preferable to the rather doubtful corn-based spirits that some English brewers were producing as a side-line. Whisky was known only in Scotland and Ireland, the cunning Celts keeping this secret to themselves.

When the troops returned with memories, and no doubt samples, of genever, some English distillers began to manufacture it. They, like the Dutch, produced it chiefly as a medicine, and this is how it was used, except by old soldiers and sailors who knew better. As evidence of this we have Samuel Pepys's entry in his diary for 10 October, 1663 : 'Sir W. Batten did advise me to take some juniper water . . . strong water made of juniper.' The doctor's recommendation had the desired effect. The interest of this entry lies in the fact that Pepys was obviously using gin in a purely medicinal capacity. Pepys was an enthusiastic and convivial imbiber and his famous diary records many drinking sessions when he was 'mighty merry'; but never on gin. Had gin been generally recognized as an alcoholic drink in his time then Samuel Pepys would surely have used it to induce the 'merriment' of which he was so fond.

This state of affairs might have continued indefinitely; it did not seem likely that gin would ever be a threat to the old established drinks, ale and beer. Nor could it conceivably compete with brandy. Gin was a Dutch drink and the Dutch were not at all popular. In 1667, the year after the Great Fire of London, the Dutch fleet had sailed, with complete immunity, up the Thames and set fire to the ships in Chatham Dockyard.

The first major change in gin's fortunes came in 1689. In the previous year Parliament had made a great effort to get rid of the unpopular Catholic king, James II. The problem was to find a formula that brought about a change without completely severing the royal continuity. Finally it was decided to offer the throne jointly to James II's daughter, Mary, and her husband, William of Orange. Enormously tactful moves were instituted, and when William landed with an army of Englishmen, Swedes and Dutch, it was pointed out that this was no 'invasion' but that he was coming by invitation. Even so, James II nearly wrecked the scheme by deciding to march against his son-in-law. There was an awkward possibility that William might have to take his father-in-law prisoner, for William had the far stronger army and James's soldiers were apt to change sides at the earliest opportunity. This embarrassment was avoided when James II was persuaded to flee to the court of Louis XIV, *his* friend and William's bitterest enemy, thus leaving the throne of England to that oddly assorted couple, William and Mary.

With the accession of a Dutchman as King William III of England there was a swift revolution in English foreign policy. Trade with France virtually ceased. The importation of brandy and French wine was effectively prohibited by means of a huge duty. A revolution in drinking habits, equal to or perhaps surpassing in importance the Glorious Revolution in politics, was about to occur.

While English foreign policy had been favourable to France, English distillers had made little headway against the overwhelming opposition of French brandy. But from 1690 onwards Parliament made a series of statutes directly encouraging the distillation of spirits from English-grown corn. First, the distilling trade was thrown open to everyone. The monopoly granted by Charles I to the Worshipful Company of Distillers to be the sole distillers in London and Westminster and within a radius of twenty-one miles beyond, was overridden. After 1690 all that a private citizen needed to do in order to gain a part of the rapidly booming trade was to post up a notice in a public place, informing the public that he intended to set up a still. He then had to wait ten days. After that, he could distil as much gin, or other spirits, as he liked.

The King led the new fashion with great enthusiasm. So great was his court's addiction to Holland's gin that the banqueting house at Hampton Court was described as a 'gin temple'. Suddenly it had become patriotic to drink gin. It was proof that one was a true Protestant. Ironically, even William's enemies – and he had many – were forced to adopt the new drink for their subversive toasts to 'the little gentleman in velvet', the mole who had made the mole-hill over which the King's horse had once stumbled.

Brandy's position was rapidly usurped; Daniel Defoe noted that the distillers had 'found out a way to hit the palate of the poor by their new-fashioned compound waters called Geneva;

so that the common people seem not to value the French brandy as usual, and even not to desire it.' But more extraordinary was the fact that gin soon began to overtake ale and beer; another contemporary writer noted that gin 'gained such universal applause, especially with the common people, that, by a moderate computation, there is more of it in quantity sold daily in many distillers' shops than of beer and ale vended in most public houses.' The outcome of this change of allegiance was inevitable: 'at country weddings, markets, burials, and the like public occasions,' wrote Andrew Fletcher, 'they are to be seen, both men and women, perpetually drunk, cursing, blaspheming and fighting each other.' In London, Henry Higden's play *The Wary Widow, or Sir Nosey Parrot* had to be abandoned on its first night and the audience sent home; by the third act the players were so drunk they were unable to speak their lines.

Because of the growing tension with France in 1691, further taxes were placed on the importation of French wine, and soon all the claret in the country was exhausted.

The following contemporary account shows the sad state of affairs that faced the dedicated wine drinker at that time:

' "Some Claret, boy!"

"Indeed, sir, we have none. Claret, sir – Lord! there's not a drop in Town. But we have the best red port."

"What's that you call red port?"

"A wine, sir, comes from Portugal; I'll fetch a pint, sir." '

This new port wine might replace claret, but what, apart from gin, was to replace brandy? The truth was that the country had relied for so long on cheap imported wines and spirits from France that little or no distilling of home-grown products had ever been undertaken.

As if to make doubly sure that the unrestricted distillation of gin could go ahead, beer duties were raised in 1694 to 4s. 9d. on strong beer and to 1s. 3d. on table beer. With wine and brandy unobtainable, and beer costing more than gin, it is hardly surprising that the consumption of gin continued to rise. In 1688,

the annual consumption in the country was around half a
million gallons. By the end of the century it had quadrupled;
and that was only a beginning.

Gin was being drunk not only by the poorer sections of the
community, who could get drunk quicker and more cheaply on
gin than on beer, but by all sections of the population.

Toasts were being drunk in gin. In the seventeenth century,
toasts were extremely serious occasions that were likely to inter-
rupt a meal at any time, and not kept merely to the end of a
formal dinner. When toasted, the person so honoured was expected, even if he were in the middle of eating, to remain utterly
immobile.

A French traveller, M. Misson, published in 1698 his
'*Memoires d'Angleterre*'. The following description of a toasting
occurs : 'If he [the person whose health is being drunk] is in
the act of taking something from a dish, he must suddenly stop,
return his fork or spoon to its place, until the other has drunk.
. . . Nothing appears so droll as to see a man, who is in the act
of chewing a morsel which he had in his mouth, or doing anything else, who suddenly takes a serious air, when a person of
some respectability drinks to his health, looks fixedly at his person, and becomes as motionless as if a universal paralysis had
seized him.'

These perpetual toasts were distracting enough when offered in
wine. In gin they were devasting.

There seemed, at the time, sound reasons for the encourage-
ment of gin production – and thus gin drinking – by the government. Distilling produced a revenue and gave farmers a market
for their corn at a time when prices were low. (In the thirty years
between 1715 and 1745 there were only three bad harvests, in
1727, 1728 and 1740.) The country at this time had a population of approximately 5,500,000, about a third of the population of present-day Greater London. The vast majority of these
people were engaged in agriculture and thus dependent in one
way or another on the corn trade. When harvests were good,

England actually produced a surplus of corn. Markets on the Continent were sought but not always found, and it was in this situation that the advantages of distilling became evident, as Daniel Defoe pointed out in the *Review* of 9 May, 1713: 'First, the corn is consum'd, which corn is our produce, pays rent for our land, employs our people, our cattle, our shipping, etc., and secondly, the importation of foreign spirits is prevented. . . . Nothing is more certain than that the ordinary produce of corn in England is much greater than the numbers of our people or cattle can consume: And this is the reason why, when markets are low abroad and no demands made for corn, that plenty which is other nations' blessing, is our intolerable burthen. . . . The distilling trade is one remedy for this disaster as it helps to carry off the great quantity of corn in such a time of plenty. . . . But in times of plenty and a moderate price of corn, the distilling of corn is one of the most essential things to support the landed interest that any branch of trade can help us to, and therefore especially to be preserved and tenderly used.'

Defoe was writing, of course, before the drinking of cheap gin become excessive. Later, when he saw the consequences of the trade he champions here, he was to change his opinion sharply.

2

Straw for Nothing

As production of gin increased, so did consumption. By 1727 the consumption of gin in England had reached 5 million gallons; by 1733 London alone was distilling 11 million gallons a year, almost twenty-three times as much as the whole country had produced in 1688.

These figures are taken from the official records and are thus unreliable in that they take no account of the production of the large number of stills churning out what would today be called 'hooch' or 'meths'. There were two kinds of distillers, malt distillers and compound distillers. The former, who produced the raw spirit, were relatively few in number and had grown very prosperous. The compound distillers, or rectifiers, catered for the masses, flavouring the malt spirits with juniper berries or aniseed and redistilling it. This process was extremely easy. All that was needed was a 'do-it-yourself' distillery kit, a burner and a receptacle to catch the distilled liquid. This liquid was known as genever and sold as such, although it often bore little or no relation to proper gin. There were a great number of compound distillers and their product was often lethal.

Unlike beer, which was sold in inns, gin could be sold everywhere. Chandlers, grocers and victuallers all sold spirits. Some shopkeepers devoted all their energies to the sale of gin: in London alone there were, by 1730, over 7,000 dram shops, i.e. shops that sold spirits alone. In 1721 the Westminster justices reported that there was no part of the City 'wherein the number of alehouses, brandy and geneva shops do not daily increase, though they were so numerous already that in some of the larger parishes every tenth house at least sells one sort or another of these liquors by retail.' The justices were perhaps erring a little on the side of caution; other authorities put the number of dram shops in their own borough of Westminster at one house in every four.

As if this wasn't enough, pedlars and hawkers roamed the streets pushing barrows containing a flagon or two of extremely bad gin. Tobacconists, and even barbers, sold gin as a side-line. In the haunts of the oldest profession of all, the 'houses of ill repute', gin sold faster than prostitutes.

The notice 'Drunk for 1d. Dead drunk for 2d. Straw for nothing' appeared outside stables, sheds and empty arches. The straw was for lying on while drinking, and for passing out on when drunk. Many never woke again. In 1723 the death rate in London overtook the birth rate and remained in that position for the next ten years.

It was the poor people in the overcrowded, insalubrious cities, particularly London, who took to the cheap 'fire-water' so recklessly. Gin was cheap, warming and soon brought happy oblivion of cold and misery. It was said to be the drink of the more sedentary trades, weavers in particular, and of women. Men doing heavy work preferred strong beer, when they could afford it. But as a justices' report in 1736 noted, 'not only the vicious and immoral give in to this practice, but also those who are in other respects sober and regular; not only one person here and there in a family, but whole families, shamefully and constantly indulge themselves in this pernicious practice.'

In the countryside the epidemic never took hold. Work there was too strenuous to allow the endless hangovers of the gin-drinking town worker. The farm worker remained faithful to his traditional, slower-working ale and beer.

It is important at this point to stress that drunkenness was not

considered a vice at this time in history. Indeed the consumption
of strong beer was one of the great British virtues. Defoe wrote
in 1702 that 'an honest drunken fellow is a character in a man's
praise', and Samuel Johnson was of the opinion that 'a man is
never happy in the present unless he is drunk'. It is odd to
reflect, as John Doxat does in *Drink and Drinking,* that 'During
the considerable period when a large number of the labouring
masses were apparently in a state of permanent intoxication, and
their rulers steadily inebriated on costlier potables, these two
social extremes – aided by a by no means abstemious commercial class, and with a hard-drinking literary and artistic coterie
to record their prowess – were building up the greatest empire
known to man. It does not seem that sobriety and national great-
ness are necessarily synonymous.'

During the early years of the eighteenth century there was
absolutely no control over the production or consumption of gin.
The only body that could have controlled at least the quality of
the gin produced, the Distillers' Company, had had all its powers
removed by Queen Anne soon after she came to the throne in
1702. Then in 1720 a provision of the Mutiny Act exempted
all retailers who were also distillers from having soldiers billeted
upon them. Innkeepers, owners of livery stables and other tradesmen were still obliged to accept soldiers. This could make a
considerable difference to profit margins, and many tradesmen
turned to distilling and selling gin in order to gain exemption
under the Act.

The campaign against gin drinking began the following year.
In April 1721 the government were concerned to discover certain 'scandalous clubs and societies of young persons' who were
rumoured to have the object of promoting blasphemy and denial
of religion. The Westminster justices were ordered to investigate.
They failed to discover the clubs, but took the opportunity to
raise their voices against the evils of spirit drinking.

The government did not respond immediately. Four years
passed. Then, on 7 October, 1725, Sir D. Dolins, Chairman of

the Middlesex Bench, in a charge to the Grand Jury, said that
the excessive drinking of gin 'is becoming so great, so loud, so
importunate, and the growing mischiefs from it so many, so
great, so destructive of the lives, families, trades and businesses
of such multitudes, especially of the lower, poorer sort of people
that I can no longer doubt but it must soon reach the ears of
our legislators.'

In the following year a committee of justices was set up to
find out how many shops were selling gin. They found that in
London alone, excluding the City and the Surrey bank, there
were 6,187 houses and shops where spirits were sold openly.
This, the justices pointed out, was probably 'very far short of the
true number', as hundreds sold gin from barrows or 'privately
in garrets, sellars, backrooms and other places. . . . All chandlers,
many tobacconists, and such who sell fruit or herbs in stalls or
wheelbarrows sell geneva. . . . In the hamlet of Bethnal Green
above forty weavers sell it.'

By 1727 even Defoe was beginning to doubt the wisdom of
allowing the unrestricted manufacture of gin. In his *Complete
English Tradesman,* published that year, he attacked the compound distillers, or rectifiers, who 'carry on their trade as if they
were always drunk, keep no books but their slate, and no pen
and ink but their chalk and tallies. . . . They are a collection of
sinners against the people, for they break almost all the known
laws of Government in the Nation.'

After George II succeeded to the throne in 1727, the first
practical steps to halt the epidemic of gin drinking were taken.
The trouble was that no one quite knew what to do. The drinking of gin had, after all, been officially encouraged for the previous fifty years. How could this be reversed?

The government finally took action in 1729. An Act was
passed requiring retailers to take out an excise licence costing
£20, a formidable sum in those days, and placing a duty of 2s.
a gallon on compound spirits. The immediate effect was to put
out of business the reputable shopkeeper who sold branded gin

only, and to put into business the bootlegger who distilled a concoction bearing only slight resemblance to gin in the back streets and sold it direct to his clients from a barrow. With the bootlegger came the protectors, the touts, the runners and collectors, all the hangers-on of an illegal trade.

As long as the Act lasted, so it became more difficult to find good gin, and easier to find the lethal kind. While the living were dying of drink, the Bishop of Cork railed against the habit of drinking to the dead. But his words carried little weight, for it was said that he only spoke in this way out of hatred for the now dead Protestant King William. Patriotic citizens, therefore, drank all the more copiously to the 'immortal memory' of William III and added still more corpses to the daily toll.

Alexander Blunt, a distilling poet or poetic distiller, however one likes to look at it, in 1729 wrote the following poem to William III, showing that Protestant patriotism, as least where drinking gin was concerned, was as strong as ever :

> Martial William drank
> Geneva, yet no age could ever boast
> A braver prince than he. Within his breast
> Glowed every virtue ! Little sign
> O Genius of *malt liquor* ! that Geneva
> Debilitates the limbs and health impairs
> And mind enervates. Men of learning famed
> And skill in medicine prescribed it then
> Frequent in recipe, nor did it want
> Success to recommend its virtues vast
> To late posterity.

Blunt was not only a good patriot and Protestant, he was a distiller, and his concern is evidence that the 1729 Act hit the established distillers hard. The farmers complained bitterly too, as the corn surplus was not being used up. In 1733 Parliament relented and repealed the Act, having found that it 'hath been a discouragement to the distilling of spirits'. In fact, more spirits were being distilled than ever before, but spirits of low quality and lethal effect. In London, during the 1730s, an estimated 11,200,000 gallons of spirits were consumed per year : 14 gallons for every adult male. The official records show that the sale of spirits rose from 3½ million gallons in 1727 to nearly 6½ million gallons in 1735.

In 1733 a new piece of legislation was brought in. Its aim was to prevent the sale of spirits outside dwelling houses, thus hitting the bootleggers. It imposed a £10 fine for the retail selling of spirits, *except in dwelling houses.* By this masterly act of miscalculation the government managed, almost overnight, to turn every single householder into a potential distiller or publican. Either he set up a still of his own, or he allowed a 'distiller' to use his home for making his spirits, thus avoiding the £10 fine – either way the cunning citizen would get all the gin he could drink, and he would get it free.

In all this talk of legislation it is important not to lose sight of the human element. The twenty-year spree had taken a terrible toll of the poor in London. M. Dorothy George, in *London Life in the 18th Century,* cites a case from the Old Bailey Session Papers of 1734 that should serve to illustrate the depths of misery to which the lowest classes in London had sunk. A young woman named Judith Dufour had a two-year-old child housed in the workhouse. The child had just been given a new set of clothes when its mother arrived to take it out for the afternoon. No sooner was she clear of the workhouse than she strangled the child, stripped off the clothes, and threw the naked corpse into a ditch in Bethnal Green. She sold the clothes for one shilling and fourpence. With the money she bought gin.

Those children who survived the vagaries of their drunken parents were little better off. In 1736 a second committee of justices from the Middlesex Bench told in their report of 'unhappy mothers [who] habituate themselves to these distilled liquors, whose children are born weak and sickly, and often look shrivel'd and old as though they had numbered many years. Others again daily give it to their children . . . and learn them even before than can go, to taste and approve this certain destroyer.'

The report of this second committee of justices, published ten years after the report of the 1726 committee, made more impression on responsible public opinion. Those who had wished to believe that the 1729 Act had curtailed the drinking of gin were forced to come to terms with the facts, for the committee presented hard statistics in their report. They found that the number of retailers selling spirits had risen from 6,187 to 7,044, and added that they had grave doubts about this figure as the returns were made by the constables, about half of whom were retailers themselves. The 'inferior trades' which sold spirits had increased to 'above fourscore . . . particularly all chandlers, many weavers, several tobacconists, shoemakers, carpenters, barbers, taylors, dyers, labourers and others.' The weavers of Bethnal Green had done so well from the trade that their numbers had more than doubled from forty in 1726 to ninety in 1736.

The committee found that credit was more or less unlimited, and labourers were encouraged to drink as much as they wanted during the week by their employers, and to settle their gin debts on pay-day at the end of the week, 'whereby at the week's end they find themselves without any surplusage to carry home to their families, which must of course starve, or be thrown on the parish.'

The authorities were becoming increasingly alarmed. It wasn't just the fact that people were being ruined and dying; but with the excessive and continuous intemperance, the population was becoming 'uppity', insolent and even rebellious. The Dutch courage found so comforting by soldiers and sailors also worked on civilians. Crowd control was difficult enough in the eighteenth century; when the crowd was dead drunk, it was impossible.

On 20 February, 1736, the Middlesex magistrates, who had met in quarter session, issued a petition to Parliament, in which they stated :

That the drinking of Geneva, and other distilled liquors, had for some years past greatly increased :

That the constant and excessive use thereof had destroyed thousands of His Majesty's subjects :

That great numbers of others were by its use rendered unfit for useful labour, debauched in morals, and drawn into all manner of vice and wickedness :

That those pernicious liquors were not only sold by distillers and geneva shopkeepers, but by many persons in inferior trades, by which means journeymen, apprentices and servants were drawn in to taste and by degrees to like, approve, and immoderately drink thereof :

That the public welfare and safety, as well as the trade of the nation, would be greatly affected by it :

That the practice was dangerous to the health, strength, peace and morals; and tended to diminish the labour and industry of His Majesty's subjects.

This was language that Parliament could understand. Instead of being referred to an ordinary committee (the quickest way of killing an idea), the petition was put before a committee of the whole House.

After very little delay, the House came to the following conclusions :

That the *low price* of spiritous liquors is the principal inducement to the excessive and pernicious use thereof :

That in order to prevent this excessive and pernicious use, a discouragement be given thereto by a duty to be laid on spirits sold by retail :

That the selling of such liquors be *restrained* to persons keeping public brandy-shops, victualling-houses, coffee-houses, ale-houses, innholders, *and to such Surgeons and Apothecaries as shall make use of it by medicine only.*

This, in itself, was a sensible suggestion, restricting the sale of spirits to publicans and the like, thereby removing the trade from the back streets. It also took care that doctors and apothecaries should revert to the medical use of gin. Had Parliament followed this lead, all might have been well, but from being too soft for years, now it suddenly became too tough. A committee, whose members included Sir Robert Walpole, the Prime Minister, and Sir Joseph Jekyll, Master of the Rolls, was ordered to prepare a Bill. Their Bill passed swiftly through its various stages and received the Royal Assent on 5 May, 1736. It declared that as from 29 September, 1736:

. . . no person shall presume, by themselves or any others employed by them, to sell or retail any brandy, rum, arrack, usquebaugh [whisky], geneva, aqua vitae, or any other distilled spiritous liquors, mixed or unmixed, in any less quantity than two gallons, without first taking out a licence for that purpose within ten days at least before they sell or retail the same; for which they shall pay down £50, to be renewed ten days before the year expires, paying the like sum, and in case of neglect to forfeit £100, such licences to be taken out within the limits of the penny post at the Chief Office of Excise, London, and at the next Office of Excise for the country. And be it enacted that for all such spiritous liquors as any retailers shall be possessed of on or after September 29th 1736, there shall be paid a duty of 20s. per gallon, and so in proportion for a greater or lesser quantity above all other duties charged on the same. .

Quite simply, the price of gin would in future be so high that only the very wealthy could buy it. It was, in fact, a form of prohibition.

In the debate Walpole had opposed the Bill, for he believed it could not be enforced. In a letter to his brother, Horace, he prophesied that the small gin shops, whose suppression was the main purpose of the Bill, would be virtually protected from prosecution by their poverty, which would discourage legal action. He was also afraid that there would be riots.

Pulteney shared Walpole's fears. He claimed that: '[The] regulation will raise great disaffection for the present government and may produce such riots and tumults as may endanger our present establishment, or at least cannot be quelled without spilling . . . blood . . . and putting an end to the liberties of the people.'

Despite the eloquence of its opponents, the Bill was passed. The Gin Act was to come into force at exactly twelve o'clock midnight on 29 September, 1736.

3

The Death and Resurrection of Madame Geneva

The speed of the Bill's enactment obviously took its opponents, rich and poor, by surprise. But immediately after it was passed a campaign started to force the government to change its plans. They had five months in which to achieve this object.

The campaign, based in London, took the form of prints, ballads and circulated letters. In early September a government informant reported that 'it is the Common Talk of the Tippling Ale houses and the little Gin Shops that Sir Robert Walpole and the Master of Ye Rolls will not outlive Michaelmas long.' The circulated letters urged distillers and retailers to celebrate 'Madame Geneva's lying-in-state' by issuing free gin to the mob on the night before the Act was due to come into force. One such letter, addressed to a Westminster distiller, urged him to be generous in his supply of liquor to his retailers and added: 'If we are English men let us show we have English spirits & not tamely submit to the yoak just ready to be fastened about our necks. Let town and country Ring with the names of Sir Robert and Sir Joseph, let them see that wooden shoes are not so easy to be worn as they imagine.'

Alexander Blunt, resorting once more to verse, tried a different tone, petitioning Sir Robert Walpole, 'statesman most profound',

To lend a gracious ear; for fame reports
That thou, with zeal assiduous, does attempt,
Superior to *Canary* or *Champagne,*
Geneva, salutiferous, to enhance;
To rescue it from hand of porter vile
And basket woman, and to the Buffet
Of lady delicate and courtier grand –
Exalt it; well from thee it may assume
The glorious modern name of Royal Bob.

On his title page he quoted an honest working-woman, who is perhaps more eloquent of the issues involved: 'We market women are up early and late, and work hard for what we have. We stand all weathers, and go thro' thick and thin. It's well known, that I was never the woman that spar'd my carcass; and if I spend three farthings now and then, in such simple stuff as we poor souls are glad to drink, it's nothing but what's my own. I get it honestly, and I don't care who knows it; for if it was not for something to cheer the spirits between whiles, and keep out the wet and cold; alackaday! it would never do! We should never be able to hold it; we should never go thorow-stitch with it, so as to keep body and soul together.'

Walpole, who was being roundly abused and threatened for an Act he had in fact opposed, remained firm. But as September approached he grew increasingly nervous. He wrote to his brother that the Jacobites were stirring up the populace 'at the approaching expiration of this darling vice' until the drunken mob was 'prepared and ready to commit any sort of mischief'.

Not everyone opposed the Act. There were many who believed that gin was rotting the moral fibre of the country, laying waste its children and causing more terrible poverty than it relieved. The Reverend James Townley attacked gin mercilessly in this set of verses:

> Gin ! cursed fiend with fury fraught,
>   Makes human race a prey,
> It enters by a deadly draught,
>   And steals our life away.
>
> Virtue and truth, driven to despair,
>   Its rages compels to fly,
> But cherishes with hellish care,
>   Theft, murder, perjury.
>
> Damn'd cup that on the vitals preys,
>   That liquid fire contains,
> Which madness to the heart conveys,
>   And rolls it through the veins.

and matched it with a companion poem extolling the virtues of beer :

> Beer ! happy produce of our isle,
>   Can sinewy strength impart,
> And wearied with fatigue and toil,
>   Can cheer each manly heart.

Another set of verses, by an anonymous supporter of the Act, shows to what extent the gin-drinking habit had been taken up by the whole population :

> Britannia this upas-tree bought of Mynheers
> Removed it through Holland and planted it here ;
> 'Tis now a stock plant of the genus wolf bane,
> And one of them blossoms in Marylebon Lane.
>
> The House that surrounds it stands first in a row,
> Two doors at right angles swing open below,
> And the children of misery daily steal in,
> And the poison they draw they denominate *Gin*.

1 'Gin Lane'. Engraving after William Hogarth.

2 A lantern-slide used at temperance lectures to show the consequences of strong drink.

3 The 'Gin Juggernath . . . its progress marked with desolation, misery and crime'. Etching by George Cruikshank.

There enter the prude, and the reprobate boy,
The mother of grief and the daughter of joy,
The serving-maid slim, and the serving-man stout,
They quickly steal in, and slowly reel out.

As the wordy battle raged between pro- and anti-prohibition-ists, the nation prepared for the fateful day, 29 September, to arrive.

The government, with a host of informers busy at their work, were fully prepared for all eventualities. Walpole doubled the guards on all government buildings and sent detachments of troops to patrol areas, such as Covent Garden, where trouble could be expected. Known agitators were kept under surveillance and a number of the more violent were detained, on various pretexts, and allowed to languish in prison for the crucial first few days after the Act took effect.

In the meantime the population was preparing for the death of 'Madame Geneva'. Great processions bearing effigies of the lady herself, gorgeously lying in state, were planned for cities like London, Plymouth, Bristol and Norwich. The effigies were huge and lascivious in appearance, and extravagant in design and construction. Madame Geneva would be lying, with her eyes closed, on a bier, or drinking, dressed in a flowing garment, on a huge bed. Attendants, usually drunk, stood around her on the float, while others, equally drunk, dragged the contraption unsteadily through the streets. The mob, brandishing glasses and sticks, marched behind, shouting for Walpole's resignation.

As the last hours of the cheap-gin era passed, the crowds pawned all their possessions to buy a final quart or gallon at the old price. Every family tried to hoard at least a little against the hard times to come. Most of the distillers had concluded that they could not continue in business under the new law, and distributed their remaining stocks free. Only two distillers indi-cated that they would take out licences and continue business. They counted on the rich being able to pay the exorbitant price

Madame Geneva being carried in procession.
Contemporary drawing

at which gin would henceforward have to sell.

The street-musicians and ballad-mongerers were hard at work, and impromptu dramas were enacted. One of the most popular was billed as being the work of 'Jack Juniper, a Distiller's Apprentice, just turned Poet' (perhaps the busy Blunt under a pseudonym?), and was entitled *The Deposing and Death of Queen Gin, with the ruin of the Duke of Rum, Marquess de Nantz, and the Lord Sugarcane, etc.* Some indication of its style and content can be gained from the following extract, recorded by Lord Kinross in his *The Kindred Spirit* :

QUEEN : The Day, my Friends, the fatal
　Day is come. . . .
　But let
　Us drink
　While yet we may. [*They give her a small glass. She throws it down.*]
　Shame on thy niggard hand,
　To fill thy Queen a glass of three go outs.
　Where is our Chamberlain,
　Sir Humphrey Thrasher?
　He better knows – mix it with carroway –
　My griefs have given me the Colic – so [*drinks*]
　Now fill to all my people.

MOB : Liberty, Property, and Gin for ever !

All through the night of 29 September the processions marched, the crowds howled, and the last pints, quarts and gallons of cheap gin were sold. Probably never in history has so much drinking been done in such a short time by so many, as on that night.

The authorities waited anxiously for the promised insurrection. The troops were reinforced at every sensitive point. The streets were patrolled by ever-larger bodies of alert and disciplined troops. Covent Garden was practically a military camp.

But nothing happened. Whether too drunk, or merely indifferent to anything but the next drink, the mob made no attempt to tear London apart brick by brick. Instead they drank until the drink ran out, then sank slowly to the pavements and into the gutters, oblivious.

In the morning the streets were littered with bodies : men, women and children sleeping off the effects of the greatest binge ever devised. Above them swung the signs of the gin shops and public houses, draped in black crape in mourning for the passing of Madame Geneva. And then, in the first hours of the new era, came the hawkers, pushing their barrows through the silent streets and offering for sale a strange-coloured liquid that tasted remarkably like gin.

A wine licence cost a few shillings, instead of the prohibitive £50 for a gin licence. Hey Presto ! Overnight the distillers became wine merchants. A strange drink, consisting of illegally distilled gin, spiced and coloured with a little wine, soon found its way onto the street barrows. This concoction, although fearful in taste and effect, could be sold almost as cheaply as the old gin. At first it was sold secretly, then openly. Chemists' shops sold it in medicine bottles, as colic and gripe waters. A variety of exotic names were coined for this new poison – 'King Theodore of Corsica', 'Sangree', 'Cuckold's Delight', 'The Cure for the Blue Devils' – but it went under the general, and perhaps inevitable name of 'Parliamentary Brandy'.

In the seven years between 1736 and 1743 only three of the £50 licences were taken out. In the same seven years the quantity of spirits sold rose to 8 million gallons a year. (Some estimates put the figure as high as 19 million gallons.) As Walpole had predicted, the Act was almost impossible to enforce. The customs officers, upon whom it fell to collect the taxes, could not cope with even the legitimate trade, and the government had to rely on that old stand-by, the paid informer, to catch the illicit retailers. These wretched men, posing as serious drinkers, would

sniff out (literally, sometimes) illicit stills and then report them
to the authorities. Their reward would usually be between 5 and
10 per cent of the fine imposed.

The magistrates, especially Colonel, later Sir Thomas, de
Veil, tried their best to enforce the Act. In the *Biography of Sir
Thomas de Veil* the anonymous author gives a poignant description of the authorities' position at this time : 'It is beyond question, that the motives upon which the law was made, were in
themselves right, and the intention of the legislature very just and
reasonable; but the mischiefs that this law was intended to
remedy had taken such deep root, and the practice of drinking
was become so general among the common people, that it certainly required great skill and caution to have eradicated it,
which this Act was so far from doing, that it really heightened
the evil by the addition of many others, as dangerous and
detestable; for on the one hand, it let loose a crew of desperate
and wicked people who turn'd informers merely for bread; and
on the other it exposed numbers of unhappy people, who before
the selling of spirituous liquors by retail became a crime, had got
a livelihood thereby, to be distressed, beggared and sent to
prison.'

Between September 1736 and July 1738, 12,000 informations
were laid against spirit retailers. There were 4,896 convictions
and 4,000 claims for the reward of £5 allowed to the informer
out of the penalty of £100. But for his fiver the informer had to
work hard and to run serious risks. The violence that the authorities had expected in 1736 broke out in the next year in isolated
incidents directed at informers, who were universally loathed.
On 28 July, 1737, an informer was stoned to death in New
Palace Yard, and three weeks later two more were murdered
by the mob. In November, when the put-upon Sir Thomas de
Veil convicted six retailers of breaking the law, the informer concerned was seized and De Veil's house threatened with destruction. In all at least five informers were killed and before long
the occupation had become so hazardous that informations

against retailers fell off, and by March 1739 they had ceased altogether.

The more intelligent of the informers soon realized that they had chosen the wrong side in this particular battle. So they changed sides. Captain Dudley Bradstreet was an indefatigable pursuer of the transgressor, bringing case after case to the notice of the authorities, earning good money and the hatred of the mob thereby. Then one day it 'occurred' to him 'to venture on that Trade', or to put it more bluntly, he realized that easier money could be made from selling gin than by informing on those doing so. Twenty years later, he recalled his exploits as a bootlegger in his delightful autobiography *The Life and Uncommon Adventures of Captain Dudley Bradstreet* (1754):

At this time the selling of Geneva in a less Quantity than two Gallons, was prohibited by Act of Parliament, and whoever presumed to do it must pay ten Pounds to the Informer, or be confined two Months in Prison, and there whipt. Most of the Gaols were full on account of this Act, and Numbers of People every Day dragged to one Prison or other for transgressing this Law.

The Mob being very noisy and clamorous for want of their beloved Liquor, which few or none at last dared to sell, it soon occurred to me to venture upon that Trade. I bought the Act, and read it over several times, and found no Authority by it to break open Doors, and that the Informer must know the Name of the Person who rented the House it was sold in. To evade this, I got an Acquaintance to take a House in Blue Anchor Alley in St Luke's Parish, who privately convey'd his Bargain to me; I then got it well secured, and laid out in a Bed and other Furniture five pounds, in Provision and Drink that would keep about two Pounds, and purchased in Moorfields the Sign of a Cat, and had it nailed to a Street Window; I then caused a Leaden Pipe, the small End out about an Inch, to be placed under the Paw of the Cat; the

End that was within had a Funnel to it.

When my House was ready for Business, I enquired what Distiller in London was most famous for good Gin, and was assured by several, that it was Mr. L-dale in Holbourn: To him I went and laid out thirteen Pounds, which was all the Money I had, except two Shillings, and told him my Scheme, which he approved of. This Cargo was sent off to my House, at the Back of which there was a Way to go in or out. When the Liquor was properly disposed, I got a Person to inform a few of the Mob, that Gin would be sold by the Cat at my Window next Day, provided they put the money in its Mouth, from whence there was a Hole that conveyed it to me. At Night I took Possession of my Den, and got up early next Morning to be ready for Custom; it was nearly three Hours before any body called, which made me almost despair of the Project; at last I heard the Chink of Money, and a comfortable Voice say, 'Puss, give me two Pennyworth of Gin'. I instantly put my Mouth to the Tube, and bid them receive it from the Pipe under her Paw, and then measured and poured it into the Funnel, from whence they soon received it. Before Night I took six Shillings, the next Day above thirty Shillings, and afterwards three or four Pounds a Day; from all Parts of London People used to resort to me in such Numbers, that my Neighbours could scarcely get in or out of their Houses. After this manner I went on for a Month, in which time I cleared upwards of two and twenty Pounds.

The wily, if not entirely praiseworthy Captain found himself a very attractive mistress, Mrs Winnett, and a few days later:

We both rose early to answer the Calls of our Friends, and help poor Puss a little. Never was Consort more charmed than mine to behold the Success of my odd Scheme, every Instant Money flowing upon me. The Street now became quite impassable, by the Numbers who came out of Curiosity to see the inchanted Cat, for so Puss was called. This Concourse of idle People had such an Effect, that my Neighbours went to their several Landlords and declared, their Houses were not tenantable unless they got the Cat-man removed; they asked who the Cat-man was, but received no other information than that he was the greatest Nuisance they ever saw or heard of.

The neighbours' complaints had the desired effect, and presently the Captain's house was visited by the authorities, out to fling him in gaol; but the astute Captain was not entirely unprepared for their visit :

We got up as early as usual, and had more to do, if possible, than ever before. About twelve o'Clock we were interrupted by the Justices, Parish Officers, Constables, and Headboroughs of Finsbury Division, who came in all their Formalities and besieged my House; they knocked at the Door, and desired Admittance; I answered, but did not appear, and told them they should not; the curious Mob and expecting Neighbours beholding all with Impatience, desirous to know the mighty Event. I requested of Mrs. W-net to go up Stairs and speech them out of a Window; she took Courage on this Occasion, dressed herself, and threw up the Sash. Greater Crouds were not to behold the Venetian Embassador to make his public Entry, than Upon this Occasion to see Mrs. W-net, with all the Glories of Youth, Beauty, and Dress in such a Place; the Sight of her captivated the Youth and Aged, from Enemies they soon became Admirers. The Word became general among them, by swearing she was the Queen of Love, she addressed them with her harmonious Voice, saying, 'Gentlemen, why do you assemble in this tumultuous manner before my Door'. The Effect of Beauty is surprising, when speaking to a rude ungovernable Mob; they instantly changed, from Jarring and Discord, to Silence equal to the Dead : She proceeded, saying,

'If you have a lawful Authority to break open my Doors, spare them not, otherwise at your Peril be it: My Manners are very inoffensive, here my Cat and I only sell the Water of Life, which if drank by any Person they shall never die, while they continue using it'. This Speech had a most incredible Effect upon five of the Hearers, who were, I suppose, enthusiastically mad before; for they instantly threw themselves on their Knees to worship her. The Justices and other Officers begged her Pardon and sneaked off, being hooted by the insulting Mob. She then disappeared, and came down Stairs.

The authorities then left him alone to rake in the money and enjoy life with Mrs W-net for another three months. By the end of that time, he recorded:

> My Scheme of a Puss, now becoming common, was prac-
> tised by many others, which greatly diminished my Business,
> and made me drop it, and turn my Head to something else.

Through the efforts of Captain Bradstreet and hundreds like him, gin was as plentiful and almost as cheap as before. The law was unenforceable. Looking back on these years in 1743, when Parliament passed a new Act, Lord Bathurst remarked: 'By their obstinacy they [the people] at last wearied the magistrates, and by their violence they intimidated those who might be inclined to make discoveries, so that the law . . . has been now for some years totally disused, nor has any man been found willing to engage in a task at once odious as endless, or to punish offences which every day multiplied, and on which the whole body of the common people, a body very formidable when united, was universally engaged.' Lord Carteret struck a similar note: 'No private man, no under officer durst inform, no magistrate durst punish, without being in danger of being De-Witted by the mob as he passed along the streets.' And the Commissioners of Excise, whose position must have been the most impossible of all, reflected this in their statement that 'policy as well as humanity obliged them to mitigate the severity of the law, which was now become odious and contemptible.'

Depending upon one's point of view, one can see the seven years between 1736 and 1743 as a triumphant demonstration that bad law cannot be imposed on an unwilling people, or as one of the worst examples of mob rule in English history, when a barbarous, drunken rabble flouted the rule of law by violence and intimidation. But whatever one's viewpoint, one must admit that gin drinking increased enormously during these years, and with it the terrible toll of human misery, poverty and wretchedness. The death rate increased, as did the numbers of children dying prematurely before the age of five, while the birth rate fell. In the three years from 1740 to 1742 there were two burials to every baptism in London, and in the twenty years from 1730 to 1749 the burials of children under five were 74.5 per cent of all the children christened.

The drinking of spirits was evidently not solely responsible for these statistics, but it was certainly the explanation most often given by contemporaries. 'The diminution of births,' wrote Corbyn Morris in 1751, 'set out from the time that the consumption of these liquors by the common people became enormous. . . . Enquire from the several hospitals in this City whether any increase of patients and of what sort, are daily brought under their care? They will all declare, increasing multitudes of dropsical and consumptive people arising from the effects of spirituous liquors.' Henry Fielding stated the case more bluntly. 'What must become of an infant,' he asked, 'who is conceived in gin, with the poisonous distillations of which it is nourished, both in the womb and at the breast?' The answer was equally simple : poverty and crime for the luckiest; the workhouse for the remainder who survived; and the graveyard for the great majority. Small wonder that gin was known as the 'great destroyer'.

4

Madame Geneva Tries to Reform

The government's attempt at prohibition came to an end in 1742. Despite some strong opposition from the bishops in the House of Lords, the Gin Act was repealed. The nation, and London in particular, had seen six years during which, in the words of Lord Islay, 'the poor had run gin-mad, the rich had run anti-gin-mad, and in this fit of madness no one would give ear to reason'.

The need for 'reason' was appreciated by all responsible men and the new Act passed in 1743 attempted to introduce this quality into the whole business of the control of drinking and drink retailing. The object of the 1743 Act was to suppress the gin shop as such, making the sale public and as far as possible respectable, and to increase the price of spirits. Annual licences costing 20s. were to be issued only to those who had an alehouse licence, and distillers were prohibited from retailing. It is a policy which, in its essence, is still with us today.

The debate in the Lords and Commons was bitter. Despite the failure of the prohibition policy introduced in 1736, many wished to retain it. Lord Lonsdale was almost lyrical in his condemnation of any 'weakening', declaring: 'The use of distilled liquors impairs the fecundity of the human race, and hinders that increase which Providence has ordained for the support of the world. Those women who riot in this poisonous debauchery are quickly disabled from bearing children, or, what is still more

39

destructive to general happiness, produce children diseased from their birth, and who, therefore, are an additional burden, and must be supported through a miserable life by the labour which they cannot share, and must be protected by that community of which they cannot contribute to the defence.'

His eloquence was in vain. The Act was passed by a substantial majority. It satisfied no one, but was at least an improvement over its precursor. The consumption of spirits did drop a little, but in 1747 there was a set-back. The compound distillers, pleading hardship and victimization, petitioned Parliament to be allowed to retail. They were allowed to do so, provided they took out a licence costing £5. Consumption rose again.

Petitions poured in to Parliament from London and the provinces, urging the government to do something to check the excessive use of spirits. Parliament dithered, changed the wording of the licences, lowered the tax on beer, but seemed unable to take really effective action. Perhaps it hoped that the gin fever would die down of its own accord. No one considered seriously improving the living standards of the poor, thus attacking the problem from the other end.

Then suddenly the tide turned. In 1751 the protests rose to a crescendo, and they were backed by two powerful pieces of propaganda, Hogarth's famous print 'Gin Lane' and Henry Fielding's essay *An Enquiry into the Causes of the Late Increase of Robbers*.

'Gin Lane' was published in 1750. It was not Hogarth's only attack on the uses or abuses of drink, but it was the most powerful of his treatments of this theme. In an earlier engraving entitled 'Strolling Actresses Dressing in a Barn', dated May 1738, he depicts a young man, apparently suffering with toothache, having gin poured down his throat by an actress. This episode is only a minor part of the engraving. In 'Gin Lane' the whole canvas is given over to the evils of excessive spirit drinking. It was said that Hogarth got the idea for the picture one Sunday when visiting an inn at Highgate with some friends. A quarrel broke out among a neighbouring party, who were consuming large quantities of gin. One of the men hit another over the head with a quart pot. The scene was irresistible to Hogarth's satirical eye; he took out his sketchbook and began to draw.

The final result was an overwhelming picture of the consequences of excessive gin drinking. In the foreground sits a drunken woman, her legs in ulcers, taking a pinch of snuff and oblivious of the fact that her child is falling to its death in the gin vault below. Other children are having gin poured down their throats, and one is left lying on the ground while its mother's corpse is carried off in a coffin. A skeletal man lies unconscious, a dog watching his empty glass. A baby is transfixed on a spike. A suicide dangles at the end of a rope. The buildings are in ruins – indicating, perhaps, that it was not only the poor who suffered, but respectable householders too – except that of the pawnbroker : he is prospering, as the family pots and pans are exchanged for drink money.

As propaganda, 'Gin Lane' was unmatched; indeed it is famous to this day.

Henry Fielding's *Enquiry* was published in 1751, two years after the publication of his best-known work, *Tom Jones.* Fielding was senior Bow Street magistrate, and with his brother John was prominent in the development of the Bow Street Runners. The *Enquiry* was only one of his works on the social problems of the times, but like 'Gin Lane' it brought the problem into sharp focus and had an immediate influence on future efforts to curtail gin drinking. The essence of Fielding's argument, and of his style, can be conveyed by one extract :

> Wretches are often brought before me, charged with theft and robbery, whom I am forced to confine before they are in a condition to be examined; and when they have afterwards become sober, I have plainly perceived from the state of the case, that the Gin alone was the cause of the trans-

gression, and have been sometimes sorry that I was obliged
to commit them to prison. . . . Gin is the principal sustenance
(if it may be so called) of more than a hundred thousan'd
people in the metropolis. Many of these wretches there are,
who swallow pints of this poison within the twenty-four hours;
the dreadful effects of which I have the misfortune everyday
to see, and smell too.

Roused by Fielding's and Hogarth's work, and spurred on by
petitions from tradesmen, manufacturers and corporations
throughout the country, Parliament passed, in 1751, a new Act.
This time it met with some success. M. Dorothy George remarks
in *London Life in the 18th Century*: 'The Act of 1751 really
did reduce the excesses of spirit drinking. It was a turning-point
in the social history of London and was so considered when this
time was still within living memory.'

The 'living memory' in question was that of a Middlesex magistrate called Collins, who wrote in the *Report on the Police of
the Metropolis* in 1817 : 'In the early part of my life (I remember
almost the time which Hogarth has pictured) when every house
in St. Giles, whatever else they sold, sold gin, every chandler's
shop sold gin, the situation of the people was terrible.'

The 1751 Act reinforced the 1743 Act, and pointedly made
it illegal for the keepers of gaols and workhouses to sell gin.
Workhouses were notorious for this habit. Twenty-five years
earlier, in 1726, the justices had this to say of them : 'And if
we may judge what will happen in other workhouses now
erecting, by what has already happened in that of St. Giles
in the Fields, we have reason to fear that the violent fondness
and desire of this liquor, which unaccountably possesses all our
poor, may prevent in great measure the good effects proposed
by them . . . it appearing by the returns from the Holborn
division that notwithstanding all the care that has been taken,
Geneva is clandestinely brought in among the poor there, and
they will suffer any punishment rather than live without it.'

Now it was to be stopped. Opposition came, perhaps not unnaturally, from the prison and workhouse authorities. They were almost as poor and wretched as the people in their charge, and their monopoly to dispense bad gin added a certain comfort to their existence.

The Act also forbade the sale of gin by chandlers. There were great numbers of chandlers in large cities. They provided the poor with their staple diet : bread, small beer and cheese. You could buy as little as a farthing's worth of goods, or half a peck (the amount that would fill a gallon pot) of coal. For years, administrators and others had been trying to stop them selling gin in small quantities. The chandler could, and did, set himself up as a distiller, a side-line that brought him, as Campbell put it in his *London Tradesmen* in 1749 : '. . . the greatest profit, and at the same time renders him the most obnoxious dealer in and about London. In these shops maid-servants and the lower class of women learn the first rudiments of drinking. . . .'

There were other interesting provisions in the Act : only publicans who paid, in London, at least £10 rent were allowed to sell gin. At the same time brewers, inn-keepers, distillers and dealers in spirits could not sit as magistrates when distillers were concerned in a case. Publicans gave credit at their risk, for debts under twenty shillings could not be recovered in law. Finally, 'Assembling to rescue offenders under the Act was made a felony, punishable with seven years transportation.'

By forbidding distillers, chandlers, grocers and workhouse-keepers to retail gin, and by increasing still further the duty on spirits, the 1751 Act removed the chief advantages of gin over, say, beer. It was no longer cheap and it could no longer be bought in a variety of often unlikely premises.

Although the Act was generally welcomed, there were those who saw it as an attack on that most sacred cow of all, British liberty. An engraving entitled 'A Modern Contrast' was circulated in 1752. On one side is a distiller being served with a writ; on the other is a publican openly serving drams to his customers. Justice is depicted lying drunk on the ground. Among the passers-by is a Frenchman, who is saying, 'If dis be Angleterre me go to France.'

But the Act did work. It made gin difficult to get, and expensive when it could be found. A further Act, on the same principles, was passed in 1756. Gradually the consumption fell, the poor presumably returning to their old favourite, beer. Equally important, the gin that was available was of a much higher quality. By 1757 the improvement was noticeable. 'The lower people of late years,' wrote Burrington, a stalwart advocate of abstinence, 'have not drunk spirituous liquors as they did before the regulations and qualifications for selling them. We do not see the hundredth part of poor wretches drunk in the streets. . . .' James Hanway, a pioneer in child care, noted two years later that 'the people themselves seem at length to have discovered, that health and pleasure, food and raiment, are better than sickness and pain, want and wretchedness.'

The reformers' cause was helped by the fact that in years of disastrous harvests the distillation of spirits from corn was sometimes prohibited. Prices then soared and consumption dropped dramatically. This happened after the scarcity of 1757, and in 1759 and 1760. Parliament was bombarded with petitions urging that prohibition on distilling should continue. The farmers pleaded that it should not. Parliament decided, however, that 'the high price of spirits hath greatly contributed to the health, sobriety and industry of the common people' and promptly increased the duty again.

As gin became more expensive, and of a higher quality, it was adopted by the middle classes. Parson Woodforde recorded, with an endearing *naïveté,* in his diary for 29 March, 1777: 'Andrews the Smuggler brought me this night about 11 o'clock a bag of Hyson tea 6 pound weight. He frightened us a little by whistling under the parlour window just as we were going to bed. I gave him some genever and paid him for the tea at 10s. 6d. per pound.'

Home consumption of British spirits dropped to a little over 2 million gallons, and between 1782 and 1784 fell to 1 million gallons as a result of yet higher duties. The death rate, too, was falling, and births increasing. Surveys undertaken at the end of the century showed that the number of retailers had also fallen considerably. In 1750, in Westminster, there were 1,300 licensed retailers and 900 unlicensed, making a total of 2,200, or one house in every eight. By 1794 there were only 957 and they were all licensed. Comparing the figures for the whole metropolis with those of 1736, the 1794 total was less than half.

In 1791 a further Act was passed, once again curtailing the number of people allowed to sell spirits. By then the excise duty on home-distilled spirits had risen from £7 7s. 0d. per tun in 1751, to £61 19s. 9d. This, more than the laws themselves, controlled the consumption of gin.

The poor still had their memories of the cheap gin era, however, and when a chance came to get some for nothing they did not hold back. In 1780, during the Gordon Riots, the mob gutted the distilleries in Holborn belonging to Thomas Langdale, a Roman Catholic. 'As yet,' wrote Horace Walpole, describing the drunken scenes outside the distilleries, 'there are more persons killed by drinking than by ball or bayonet.' Langdale reputedly had 120,000 gallons in his cellars. His gin, however, was only a diversion; he was attacked on account of his religious beliefs.

In 1795, the Speaker of the House of Commons, in a speech at the Bar of the Lords, told the Upper House that all tax restrictions had been lifted from the brewing trade, so as to give it 'a decided advantage over the distilling, and thereby, discourage the too frequent and immoderate use of spirituous liquors, a measure which must conduce to sobriety, tranquillity, and content, and under which the people, encouraged in regular industry, and the consequent acquisition of wealth, must feel the blessings.' It seemed that in the great battle between gin and beer, beer had finally emerged the winner.

'The Mob'.
Drawing by H. K. Browne

But gin had not suffered a total defeat. If it could not be the popular drink of the working man, it could do better. And by the end of the century, gin, if not yet the respectable drink it was to become, had reached a sufficiently recognized position to be included in A. Cooper's *The Complete Distiller,* published in 1797. His tone gives little hint of the horrors of the past:

There was formerly kept in the apothecaries' shops a distilled spirituous water of juniper; but the vulgar being fond of it as a dram, the Distillers supplanted the apothecaries, and sold it under the name of geneva. The common sort however is not made from juniper-berries as it ought to be, but from oil of turpentine; the method of which we shall give in the sequel of this chapter.

Juniper-berries are a roundish fruit, of the size of a pea. They wither and wrinkle in the drying, and we meet with them variously corrugated, and usually covered with a bluish resinous dust when fresh. They should be chosen fresh, plump, full of pulp, and of a strong taste and smell. They are usually imported from Germany, though we have plenty of the trees in England. It is but small with us, rarely rising to more than three or four feet in height, and scarce ever exceeding five or six. Some of the juniper shrubs are males, some females of the same species; the male shrubs produce in April or May a small kind of juli with apices on them very large, and full of farina; the females produce none of these juli but only the berries, which do not ripen till the second year, and then do not immediately fall off, so that it is no uncommon thing to see three sets of berries, or the berries of three different years at once on the same tree.

If you make use of English berries, let them be fully ripe before they are gathered; and in order to preserve them, spread very thin on a boarded floor, leaving the windows and doors open, and turn them once a day till they are dry; after which pack them up in barrels, so that no air may come to them, and they will keep good all the year. Some, when they are dry, throw them altogether in a heap in a corner of the room, where they continue till wanted for use: but the berries will not keep so well by this method, as by being packed in casks, they are subject to contract a mouldiness, which will give a taste to the goods greatly to their disadvantage.

Some Distillers as soon as their berries are gathered, put them into casks, and cover them with spirits of wine; by this method the berries are indeed well preserved, without any danger of contracting an ill smell, which they are very apt to do by the other methods unless the greatest care be taken; but then it must be remembered, that the spirit will extract great part of their essential oil in which their virtues consist, and consequently the berries themselves will be rendered of little value. If, therefore, you preserve your berries in this manner, you should put into each cask or jarr, only the quantity you use of one charge of your still; and when you have occasion to use them, put both the spirits and berries into your alembic.

Thus your berries will be finely preserved, without any loss either of their essential oil, or the spirits made use of to preserve.

Recipe for making ten Gallons of Geneva

Take of juniper-berries three pounds; proof spirit ten gallons; water four gallons. Draw off by a gentle fire till the faints begin to rise, and make up your goods to the strength required with clean water.

The Distillers generally call those goods which are made up proof by the name of royal geneva; for the common sort is much below proof, ten gallons of spirit being sufficient for fifteen gallons of geneva. Nay, what is generally sold at the common alehouses is made in the following manner:

Take of the ordinary malt spirits ten gallons; oil of turpentine two ounces; bay salt three handfuls. Draw off by a gentle fire till the faints begin to rise, and make up your goods to the strength required with clean water.

In this manner is the common geneva made, and it is surprizing that people should accustom themselves to drink it for pleasure.

There is a sort of this liquor called Holland's geneva, from its being imported from Holland, which is greatly esteemed.

The ingredients used by the Dutch are, however, the same

as those given in the first recipe of this chapter, only instead of malt spirit they use French brandy. In the first part of this Treatise we have sufficiently shewn the nature of French brandy, and in what its excellence consists; and, also, that by the help of a clean spirit, cordial waters may be made with the same goodness as those drawn with French brandy. If therefore the Distiller be careful in distilling and rectifying his malt spirit, he may make geneva equal to that of the Dutch, provided it be kept to a proper age; for all spirituous liquors contract a softness and mellowness by age, impossible to be imitated by art.

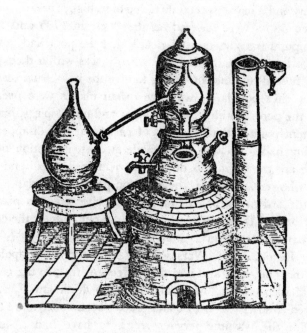

An early distillery

5

The Coming of the Gin Palaces

As the eighteenth century drew to a close, gin was in a state of flux. Beer had regained its position as the staple alcoholic drink of the poor, leaving gin in a no-man's-land between its old notoriety and a new respectability, due to its higher price.

When duties were lowered, as they were in 1785 and 1786, consumption statistics showed clearly that the poor had not lost their taste for 'Madame Geneva' when it was within their price range. Indeed it would be wrong to give the impression that the days of gin's popularity with the urban masses were over for good; the poor continued to drink gin and other spirits, but the important point is that the days of *cheap* gin had disappeared. Drinking habits became more moderate. An indication of the change are the comments of an American visitor to London in 1805, who remarked that 'the common people in England drink but little ardent spirits, because its excessive dearness places it almost beyond their reach.' He added, 'in our country the effects are dreadful, because every man can procure it.'

The Revolutionary Wars with France, and the Napoleonic Wars that followed, also had their effect. At first, in the general state of suspense and national effort, the drink laws were not enforced as strictly as before and grocers began once more to sell gin. But the wartime fervour seems to have had a curious sobering effect on the population. Drunkenness was no longer regarded as a fashionable or natural condition, and began to be condemned as a distateful state to be in, or even as a disgusting vice. As early as the 1770s Adam Smith was claiming that drunkenness was 'by no means the vice of people of fashion', and by the 1830s most people shared his views. In 1835 the *Eclectic Review* was bold enough to state bluntly that drunkenness was 'now a *vulgar* vice'. This important change in thinking began in the world of fashion at one end of society, and of labour at the other, but its chief proponents were to be found among the emerging middle classes. Societies for the Reformation of Manners, which had been active around 1700, surfaced again with renewed vigour in the 1780s. Their targets were 'all manner of vice, profaneness and immorality', which included drunkenness.

Another important development at this time was the introduction of a new kind of coffee shop. This was both a cause and a result of the growing sobriety of the London workman. The tax on coffee was reduced in 1808 and coffee became a favourite breakfast drink for working men. It is important to remember that water at this time was generally unsafe to drink, even in the countryside. A 'water drinker', like Benjamin Franklin, who had tried to convert London printers to water in 1725, was regarded as an eccentric. Thus, to quench one's thirst one relied on intoxicants whose water had been pumped from deep wells, or on hot beverages whose water had been boiled. Tea had been popular in the eighteenth century among those who could afford it, but from the 1820s to the 1850s the consumption of coffee rose faster than that of tea. The budget of 1825 reduced duties on coffee yet further and there was a rapid expansion in coffee shops. By 1830 coffee was almost as cheap as beer, costing 3d. or 4d. a pint to beer's $4\frac{1}{2}$d. to 6d. per quart. According to Francis Place in 1835, these coffee shops were 'the means of great improvement to the working people'.

Although the general drunkenness of the first thirty years of the nineteenth century was less alarming than that of a hundred years before it was still a serious problem. Drinking was an important part of life and drinking customs were interwoven into the fabric of society to an astonishing extent. Almost every trade had traditions involving massive drinking sprees on special occasions, such as when an apprentice joined a firm, a system known as 'drinking usages'. In 1839 John Dunlop, a Greenock magistrate, published a survey of these customs entitled *The Philosophy of Artificial and Compulsory Drinking Usages in Great Britain and Ireland*. He described in detail 300 usages in 98 different trades. In Scotland, for instance, miners were given a gallon of whisky when a new seam of coal was discovered, while the footing for admission to a skilled trade ranged from ten shillings in the cotton trade to seven pounds among calico-printers. These usages were rigorously enforced and the consequences of non-payment were dire; in the furniture trade a boy who refused to pay had a heavy cloth thrown over him from behind, 'his hands are then tied and he is laid on his face along a bench, his shoes are taken off and he is sharply beat on the soles of his feet with a flat board. He remains after this the object of unrelenting abuse and spite.'

Lest one might be tempted to suppose that this system was confined to labourers and artisans, it is worth noting that the justices had similar customs involving the payment of a guinea to any justice who should 'acquire any title of honour or dignity, or be married', and that this was in addition to 'colt money' which was paid by the justices when they first took their seats on the bench. Other professions had similar traditions.

The price structure pertaining at this time dictated that most of the footing money was spent on ale and beer, although mentions of gin are not infrequent. In Scotland and Ireland spirits, in the form of whisky, still reigned supreme, however, and this may account for these countries' usurpation of London's traditional role as the centre of drunkenness in the kingdom. An American visitor in the 1820s was of the opinion that 'the Irish people were the most drunken race on the face of the earth'. Accounts of Donnybrook Fair, held on the outskirts of Dublin every August, would seem to bear him out : 'One third of the public lay, or rolled about drunk. Others . . . screamed, shouted and fought. The women rode about, sitting two or three upon an ass . . . smoked with great delight and coquetted with their sweethearts.' Only the Scots could equal them; here is a press report from 1830; describing a coming-of-age party for a wealthy young gentleman :

The work of jollification went on briskly. In a very short time hundreds were in a state of deep intoxication and hand-barrows and carts were . . . put in requisition to convey them to their several habitations. On the roads in every direction people were found lying helpless. One man states that between Bannockburn and Stirling, he loosened the neckcloths of no less than eight individuals in danger of suffocation. Around the table men, women and children, were to be seen stagger-ing about in inimitable confusion, tumbling over each other and lying by scores in every direction. On Sunday morning, parties were out in all directions looking for relations and friends and removing them from the highways that they might not be observed by people going to church.

The policy of the government remained virtually unchanged. It encouraged the consumption of beer at the expense of gin and other spirits. In 1830 the Sale of Beer Act was passed, giving anyone the right to sell beer if he paid two guineas for a licence, and abolishing the duty. A few Members resisted but the majority of the House were enthusiastic. Henry Brougham saw the Act as giving the people 'good beer instead of bad spirits . . . giving to them what under present circumstances might be called a moral species of beverage.'

The results of this piece of legislation were, of course, re-markably similar to those of that designed to encourage distil-ling a hundred years earlier. Thousands flocked to obtain licences, and many more to patronize the new establishments that sprung up. In Liverpool fifty beer shops were opening every day during the period immediately following the enforcement of the Act. By the end of 1830 there were 24,000 beer shops in England and Wales; six years later there were 46,000. The number of public houses also grew, although more slowly, to a total of 56,000 by 1836. Thus for a population of about 15 million people in England and Wales, there were now 100,000 places at which one could obtain an intoxicating drink.

Part of the intention of the 1830 Act, in allowing anyone to open a beer shop, was to break the monopoly of the large, powerful brewers and their 'tied houses'. This it signally failed to do. The brewers in fact prospered as a result, and where they did not they sought to compete with the new licensees by revamping their old public houses and transforming them into magnificent edifices that could not but tempt the thirsty passerby. Those brewers and publicans who could not afford the transformation competed by opening additional premises to sell spirits, to compensate for their falling profits from beer. The result was that consumption of spirits was once again on the increase.

In the evidence given to the Select Committee on Drunkenness in 1834, there is a marvellous description by a London grocer of what happened to a dingy, dirty pub, with only one doorway, that stood opposite his home in Tothill Street. Almost overnight it became 'a splendid edifice, the front ornamented with pilasters supporting a handsome cornice . . . the doorways were increased to three, and each of those eight to ten feet wide . . . and the doors and windows glazed with very large single squares of plate glass, and the gas fittings of the most costly description.' When the transformation was complete, 'notice was given by placards taken round the parish; a band of music was stationed in front . . . and when the doors were opened the rush was tremendous; it was instantly filled with customers and continued so till midnight.'

The gin palace had arrived.

Soon there were thousands of these magnificent buildings. The façade of luxury was maintained throughout. The managers were selected for the joviality of their features, the barmaids for their prettiness. In winter, fires burnt in the open hearths, bringing warmth and happiness to the customers. A variety of temptingly-named drinks were available: 'Prime double-stout, mild ale, best cordial gin, cream of the valley, Old Tom, pineapple rum, genuine Scotch whisky, best French brandy, rum-shrub . . .' The scene was Dickensian, and of course Dickens did not neglect to describe it. Here is his picture of a gin palace from *Sketches by Boz*:

You turn the corner. What a change! All is light and brilliancy. The hum of many voices issues from that splendid gin-shop which forms the commencement of the two streets opposite; and the gay building with the fantastically ornamented parapet, the illuminated clock, the plate-glass windows surrounded by stucco rosettes, and its profusion of gas-lights in richly-gilt burners, is perfectly dazzling when contrasted with the darkness and dirt we have just left. The interior is even gayer than the exterior. A bar of French-polished mahogany, elegantly carved, extends the whole width of the place; and there are two side-aisles of great casks, painted green and gold, enclosed within a light brass rail, and bearing such inscriptions as 'Old Tom, 549'; 'Young Tom, 360'; 'Samson, 1421' – the figures agreeing, we presume, with 'gallons', understand. Beyond the bar is a lofty and spacious saloon, full of the same enticing vessels, with a gallery running round it, equally well furnished. On the counter, in addition to the usual spirit apparatus, are two or three little baskets of cakes and biscuits, which are carefully secured at the top with wicker-work, to prevent their contents being unlawfully abstracted. Behind it are two showily-dressed damsels with large necklaces, dispensing the spirits and 'compounds'. They are assisted by the ostensible proprietor of the concern, a stout

Outside a gin palace.
Engraving after a drawing by George Cruikshank

coarse fellow in a fur cap, put on very much on one side to
give him a knowing air, and to display his sandy whiskers to
the best advantage.

The two old washerwomen, who are seated on the little
bench to the left of the bar, are rather overcome by the head-
dresses and haughty demeanour of the young ladies who
officiate. They receive their half-quartern of gin and pepper-
mint with considerable deference, prefacing a request for 'one
of them soft biscuits', with a 'Jist be good enough, ma'am'.

The reformer in Dickens led him to conclude his sketch with
these words:

Gin-drinking is a great vice in England, but wretchedness
and dirt are a greater; and until you improve the homes of

the poor, or persuade a half-famished wretch not to seek relief in the temporary oblivion of his own misery, with the pittance which, divided among his family, would furnish a morsel of bread for each, gin-shops will increase in number and splendour. If Temperance Societies would suggest an antidote against hunger, filth, and foul air, or could establish dispensaries for the gratuitous distribution of bottles of lethe-water, gin-palaces would be numbered among the things that were.

Dickens's famous illustrator, Cruickshank, also attacked gin in his work. His illustration of the Gin Juggernath, with its ornamental gin-palace decor and its huge barrel-wheels crushing to death its frenzied worshippers, became as well-known as Hogarth's 'Gin Lane'.

Gin, it seemed, was enjoying a renaissance. Consumption was rising, and Madame Geneva's most faithful followers, the urban poor, were returning to her, lured by the glitter and glamour of the gin palaces. England was undergoing a transformation. The age of the Industrial Revolution was beginning. The traditional patterns of life were being eroded as new towns and cities sprung up, and the people flocked from the countryside to work in the factories. Gin had always been the drink of the urban worker; now there were thousands of them, the 'working classes', all over the country. They lived in drab, monotonous rows of identical houses and it is easy to understand the attraction of the warm, bright, exciting gin palaces, which seemed to offer gaiety and laughter, and, above all, release from the cares of the moment. It was almost as though the clock had been put back a hundred years. George Wilson, the Tothill Street grocer, spoke in his evidence of a scene that might have inspired a new 'Gin Lane':

I arose about seven o'clock and looked from my bedroom at the gin-palace opposite to me. I saw it surrounded with customers. Amongst them I saw two coal-porters . . . with women who appeared to be their wives; and a little child, about six or seven years old. They got to the bar and came out again in a short time, one of the women so intoxicated as to be unable to walk; she went against the door-post, and then fell flat on the pavement, with her legs partly in the shop and her person exposed; the three who were with her attempted to raise her, but they were so intoxicated as to be unable to perform that task. . . . After a considerable time they succeeded . . . and placed her against the door-post . . . the little child endeavoured to arouse her by smacking her on the legs and on the face, but she appeared quite insensible.

His words were much-quoted, and were used as potent propaganda by a new force, the temperance movement, that although ultimately unsuccessful, was to put paid to any fears – or hopes – of a new epidemic of gin drinking on eighteenth-century lines.

6

The T-T-Totallers

The temperance movement began in the United States about
1770, and by the 1830s American temperance ideas and tracts
were spreading to Britain. There had been British abstainers
before this, but they had tended to act alone or in the form of
obscure sects like the Cowherdites, who renounced all 'animal
food' and intoxicating drink. Only in the 1830s did organized,
non-religious temperance organizations emerge as a powerful
force.

A number of factors contributed to the appearance of a temperance movement at this time. Attacks on drunkenness had
been made for some years as part of a more general attempt
to propagate a middle-class style of life. Religious and secular
opinion-formers had been campaigning for sobriety during the
1820s, and these had included a 'sober and self-improving aris-
tocracy of labour' who preached temperance for purely practical,
secular reasons. Non-intoxicating drinks were at last beginning
to equal alcohol in cheapness and accessibility. And evangelists,
both inside and outside the established church, were ready with
the impetus and the techniques necessary to launch a nationwide
humanitarian movement. Increasing industrialization and urban-
ization provided the necessary conditions for organizing a mass
movement – cheap printing and increased mobility – and also
contributed to temperance ideology : the reformers saw their
movement as part of a general attack on ignorance and back-

wardness.

The early temperance reformers were 'moderationists', attacking the drinking of spirits but not of all alcohol. They were not total abstainers, and supplied beer in their reading rooms and coffee houses. The movement began in Ireland, where John Edgar was the anti-spirits pioneer, and in Scotland, led by John Dunlop. By the end of 1830 there were 130 societies in Scotland, with a membership of 25,000. The impetus spread quickly to England, being particularly successful in Yorkshire and Lancashire, and in November 1830 the London Temperance Society was founded, becoming the British and Foreign Temperance Society in the following July. Members pledged themselves to abstain from all spirits 'except for medicinal purposes' and to 'discountenance the causes and practice of intemperance'. Brian Harrison in *Drink and the Victorians* describes the British and Foreign Temperance Society as a 'London-based reforming society on the traditional evangelical model. It paraded great names, and within a year claimed the Bishop of London as president, with four peers and four bishops among its vice-presidents'.

The Society was criticized from the first. Its aristocratic and Anglican structure was not popular with provincial nonconformists, and what was worse, a mere switch from spirits to beer or wine seems to have done little to promote sobriety. There were arguments about whether spirits were in fact that much more intoxicating than beer or wine, and the more cynical pointed out that some of the Society's members became more drunk on beer than non-members on gin. The Society had also failed to take account of regional variations; in many areas spirit drinking was almost unknown, thus members would happily pledge to eschew spirits while continuing to down quarts of potent home-brewed beer or cider.

Meanwhile, in Preston, Lancashire, the inevitable was taking place. Joseph Livesey, a local cheesemonger, nonconformist and reformer, initiated a 'total' pledge, promising abstinence from

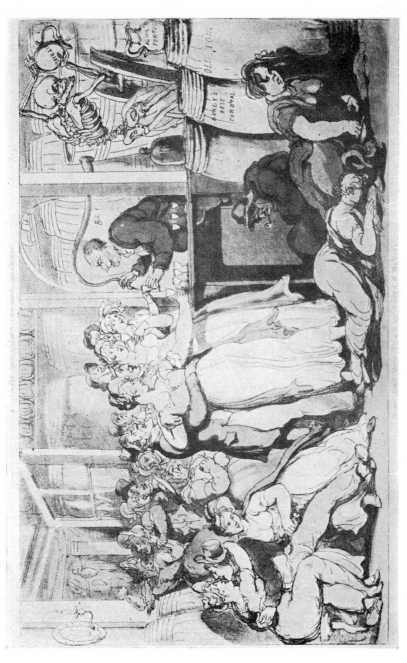

4 'The Dram Shop' by Thomas Rowlandson. Plate from 'The Dance of Death', 1815.

5 and 6 Advertisements for gin from the Cocktail Age (*left*) and from the present day.

'The Raving Maniac and the Driv'ling Fool'.
Etching by George Cruikshank

all alcoholic drinks. Livesey considered that 'the liberty to take wine and beer in moderation' was 'a fatal source of backsliding'. On 23 August, 1832, he and six other men signed this pledge: 'We agree to abstain from all liquors of an intoxicating quality, whether ale, porter, wine or ardent spirits, except as medicine.' Livesey was a radical and was prepared to employ radical methods. Reformed drunkards, carrying the symbols and wearing the clothes of their trades, appeared at temperance meetings, telling from their own experience of the horrors of drink in language that all could understand. It was one of these men who gave the total abstinence movement its name. In September 1833 Dicky Turner told an enthusiastic audience at the Preston Temperance Society, 'I'll have nowt to do wi' this moderation, botheration pledge', and becoming carried away, he began to stutter, 'I'll be reet down and out t-t-total for ever and ever!' At this Livesey leapt to his feet, exclaiming 'That shall be the name.' From then on the total abstainers were known as teetotallers. They set out to educate the whole country in their principles.

The moderationists had little chance. Between 1834 and 1836 the teetotallers gained control of the temperance movement. Their speakers were indefatigable and persuasive and their propaganda techniques were often revolutionary. The temperance movement lost its middle-class image as the poor began to take the pledge in ever-increasing numbers. On teetotal platforms stood men like William Smith, a 'wild man of the woods' in appearance, who told his audience that after renouncing liquor, 'I soon experienced such an improvement in my sight that my spectacles were unnecessary, my rheumatism and other complaints disappeared, and I grew so much more bulky that I had to make a loop of a rosin and to lengthen the waistband of my trousers.' This was not the sort of lecture that the ladies of the British and Foreign Temperance Society enjoyed. But there can be no doubt that it was a successful approach. Henry Anderton, a teetotaller, noted in 1834: 'Where none but privileged and educated people are permitted to speak . . . the societies are dying or dead. . . . Where uneducated, reformed drunkards have full liberty to tell their round unvarnished tale, and where abstinence, unqualified abstinence is held forth . . . those societies are progressing with a glorious rapidity.'

In the provinces the teetotallers swept all before them. Only in London did the Society fight a hopeless rearguard action. By 1848 it had disappeared.

Teetotalism was a radical movement and in its early days it made no impression in Parliament. Nor, indeed, did it wish to, its leaders believing that a dramatic change in national habits could be secured without resort to legislation. In turn, Parliament seemed indifferent to the temperance movement. Joseph Brotherton, the first teetotal MP, was notorious in the House for invariably moving for adjournment at midnight, a proposal 'met with a chorus of cheers, groans, hootings, cock-crowings, bellowings, and other discordant cries'. His teetotalism was regarded as merely another eccentricity of an already eccentric man.

The anti-spirits movement had a more powerful Parliamentary champion in James Silk Buckingham, although his speeches and imaginative schemes for social reform were also greeted with derision. He signed the pledge in 1832, and two years later pressed for a Parliamentary inquiry into drunkenness. Despite opposition from all sides he persisted and a Committee was set up in June 1834 under his chairmanship.

Ridiculed in the London press, where the Committee was dubbed 'The Drunken Committee', Buckingham and his colleagues concentrated their attack on gin. They put the blame for the nation's drunkenness entirely on spirit drinking and made no reference to beer drinking. First-hand evidence was heard about men who had pawned their clothes for gin and women who had stripped off their petticoats in the gin shop in order to purchase more liquor. They also heard how an estimated 30 per cent of parish relief, often known as 'gin money', was spent on gin the same day it was given.

In its report the Committee recommended several 'immediate' remedies. All licences should be renewed annually under magistrates' supervision, and fewer licences should be granted. Closing hours should be uniform and earlier. Spirit shops should be open to public view and the sale of spirits, except in inns, should be entirely separate from the sale of other goods. The spirit ration in the armed forces should be abolished. Wages should cease to be paid out in public houses. Parks, reading-rooms and libraries should be established. The 'ultimate' remedy, to be applied when public opinion was ready, was the complete prohibition of the manufacture, importation or sale of spirits.

Public opinion was not ready for any of Buckingham's proposals. The Report met with scorn in Parliament. *Hansard* recorded: 'The Clerk read the Report, which was accompanied by much cheering and laughter.' Buckingham even had to fight hard to get his Parliamentary colleagues to allow the Report to be printed. When it was, the press seized on it with delight. *John Bull* proposed that the Committee should report every month to keep the nation merry, and other newspapers were equally mocking.

The project failed. But many of the ideas put forward in the Report were later adopted and it became the textbook of the teetotal movement and was widely quoted in the years that followed. Buckingham continued to campaign and was prominent on temperance platforms until his death in 1855. As a contemporary noted, Buckingham was not merely 'before his day, he was above it'.

Meanwhile, in the provinces and in Ireland and Scotland, the teetotallers continued to campaign. They were not universally welcomed: James Teare's legendary journey through England, spreading the teetotal gospel, was attended by riotous scenes as he was attacked by drunkards and even by moderationists. Teetotallers were the object of public ridicule and were barred from certain halls and business premises. In response they established their own halls, friendly societies and hotels where alcohol was not available. The aim was to create a drink-free alternative society.

Teetotalism's first decade, 1832-42, was probably the time of its greatest successes, as thousands flocked to take the pledge. But by the 1840s the opposition was hardening. Anti-teetotal tracts began to appear, to counter the stream of propaganda that poured from the teetotal presses. *A medical, moral and Christian dissection of teetotalism,* published in 1846, went through eleven editions. Thomas Smeeton, one of teetotalism's best-known converts, reneged on his former colleagues and produced a long pamphlet in 1849 entitled *Confessions of a Convert from Teetotalism to Temperance*. In 1851 Charles Dickens came out against the teetotallers, publishing a satirical account of a temperance march in his magazine, *Household Words*.

The 1850s began promisingly for the movement, however. Alcohol was banned from the Great Exhibition of 1851. Provincial teetotallers marched to the Exhibition, and then held a fête at the Zoo which was attended by 25,000 people. The profits were used to found the London Temperance League.

A more important new organization was the United Kingdom Alliance for the Suppression of the Traffic in all Intoxicating Liquors, founded in 1853. Its aim was the complete prohibition of the *sale* of all intoxicating drink. Within four years it had 50,000 members. The only way that the Alliance could achieve its aim was through legislation, so its members devoted much of their energy to lobbying MPs and trying to steer public opinion in the direction of prohibition by bludgeoning it with propaganda. Every aspect of the 'accursed trade' – even inn signs – was attacked in one Alliance pamphlet or another. The publicans returned the fire in pamphlets of their own.

Part of the Alliance creed was that their hoped-for prohibition would only stop the sale of drink, one would still be permitted to brew one's own beer or import one's own wine. This roused the fury of those working for total abstention. As Joseph Livesey pointed out, 'If it be right to brew your own beer, I cannot see how it can be wrong for your neighbour of the Royal Hotel to brew it for you and take pay for it.' 'Buyers are equally to blame with sellers and forty times as numerous,' he said later. The argument ended in a bitter libel suit between John B. Gough, a British-born American and a famous temperance orator for the London Temperance League, and Frederick Lees, a supporter of the Alliance. Their feud did the temperance cause great harm.

One issue that united the temperance movement was Sunday drinking. Members of all persuasions saw it as an affront to

God and a temptation to man. Since 1828 the law had required public houses to close during the hours of church services, but it was widely ignored. In 1848 the 1839 Metropolitan Police Act, which had closed all public houses within a fifteen-mile radius of Charing Cross from midnight on Saturday till 1 p.m. on Sunday, was extended to include the whole of England and Wales. Scotland had the Forbes-Mackenzie Act, which from June 1845 had closed all licensed premises for all of Sunday, except for hotels catering for travellers, who were thought to need liquid sustenance after the rigours of Victorian travel. It was a law on this basis that English reformers wanted.

7

The Bona Fide Traveller

In 1853 the House of Commons appointed a Select Committee on the control of places of public entertainment. Four years earlier a similar committee of the House of Lords, under the chairmanship of the Earl of Harrowby, had also investigated the drink problem and found to its distress that 'The consumption of ardent spirits has, from whatever causes, far from diminished; and that the comforts and morals of the poor have been seriously impaired.' It also discovered that since the introduction of the Beer Act the number of houses selling intoxicating liquors had grown from 88,930 to 123,396. Worse still, only one twelfth of these brewed their own beer. The rest, as often as not, sold either inferior beers or concentrated openly on the sale of gin. The committee's report, although much discussed, had produced no legislative action. The Commons committee was to fare better.

The Villiers Committee, so called after its president C. P. Villiers, sat for forty-one days. It heard evidence from a wide variety of interested parties, some of which was startling. Many publicans, for example, revealed that they added gin or other spirits to their beer in order to give it a 'kick'. One such 'recipe' went as follows: 'To a barrel of porter [add] 12 gallons of liquor, 4 lbs. of foots [coarse sugar], 1 lb. of salt; and sometimes to bring a head up, a little *vitriol, cocculus indicus,* also a variety of things very minute.' A potent beverage indeed!

The Villiers Committee reported in 1854, recommending shorter Sunday opening hours for public houses. A Bill was rushed through Parliament and on 7 August, 1854 the new Sale of Beer Act became law. This Act closed public houses and beer shops from 2 p.m. to 6 p.m. on Sunday afternoons, and obliged all public houses to close at 10 p.m. They could not open again until 4 a.m. the following morning.

Once again, Parliament had taken the public by surprise. On Sunday, 13 August, crowds besieged the public houses, many of them claiming to be travellers. (Bona fide travellers were exempted from the Act's provisions, as in Scotland.) 'In several places,' reported *The Times,* 'persons on being refused pretended that they were seized with cholera [for which the traditional remedy was brandy], but none of those were served.' The police and magistrates, however, were delighted. G. A. Beckett, the Southwark Police Court magistrate, wrote to *The Times* 'that on the Monday mornings before the Act, the business of the Court was greater than on other days, but that since, it had only averaged two cases of drunkenness for each Sunday.'

In the months that followed many minds were exercised over the problem of what constituted a 'bona fide traveller'. A man who walked from the West End to Hampstead was told by a magistrate that he qualified, but that had he walked from the East End to Piccadilly he would not have done. 'What does a traveller look like?' wondered *The Times* in September. 'Is he a dirty man, with muddy or with dusty boots, according to the season? Surely nothing is simpler than for an impostor to step into a puddle or kick up a cloud of dust around him just as he makes an application at the inn door?' The newspaper concluded that 'unless an available test can be suggested the restriction ought to be universally enforced or entirely abolished.'

The populace seemed to be in favour of the latter option, and when Lord Robert Grosvenor introduced a Bill in 1855 to prevent all Sunday trading their anger boiled over. Massive demonstrations took place in Hyde Park, and the wealthy citizens driving in the park were pelted with mud and stones. Grosvenor's house was besieged, together with those of other prominent people, and police reinforcements were brought in to put down the rioters.

Another committee was convened, and recommended an extension of Sunday licensing hours to 11 p.m. On Tuesday, 14 August, 1855, the Sale of Beer Act became law. It was a major defeat for the teetotallers.

The bone fide traveller became a national joke, with the growth of rail travel greatly aiding the determined drinker. In 1872 Parliament laid down that one must travel at least three miles to qualify, and in 1893 that a journey was not 'bona fide' if its object was to gain refreshment. But evasion was now a popular game and ingenious ruses were thought up. Often a single day-return rail ticket was passed from hand to hand as each new applicant justified his claim to a drink. Mr Pooter, the hero of George and Weedon Grossmith's fictitious but carefully observed *Diary of a Nobody,* was not so successful :

We arrived; and as I was trying to pass, the man in charge of the gate said : 'Where from?' I replied : 'Holloway'. He immediately put up his arm, and declined to let me pass. I turned back for a moment, when I saw Stillbrook, closely followed by Cummings and Gowing, make for the entrance. I watched them, and thought I would have a good laugh at their expense. I heard the porter say : 'Where from?' When, to my surprise, in fact disgust, Stillbrook replied : 'Blackheath', and the three were immediately admitted.

All four had come from Holloway.

The 1855 Sale of Beer Act finally convinced the United Kingdom Alliance that there was no chance of Parliament imposing a policy of total prohibition throughout the country. They decided to press instead for a Permissive Bill, which would allow each district to vote, if it wished, to suppress all licences within its borders. The Bill, moved by Sir Wilfrid Lawson in 1864, proposed that a two-thirds majority of 'owners and occupiers of property' should take this decision. It was thrown out by a huge majority, but Lawson introduced it again and again in later years, never with any success.

Gladstone, who as Chancellor in 1860 had introduced, in the name of Free Trade, a Bill that flooded the country with cheap wine from France, Spain and Portugal, in 1870 promised legislation to reform the whole licensing system. In 1871 the Home Secretary, Henry Bruce, introduced a Licensing Bill which proposed that licences should be awarded in relation to population density. Where the number of licences exceeded one per 1,000 inhabitants in towns, or one per 600 inhabitants in rural areas, a three-fifths majority of ratepayers would be given the power to reduce this figure. The granting of additional licences would be subject to 'local option'.

The Bill satisfied no one. Many saw it as an attack on the freedom of the individual. A bishop declared that he 'would rather see England free than England sober'. The drink trade attacked it ceaselessly, and the teetotallers condemned it for its mildness. Gladstone hastily withdrew it and replaced it with a much milder measure, the Intoxicating Liquor (Licensing) Act 1872, which prohibited the sale of spirits for consumption on the premises by children under sixteen, and laid down new opening hours. But his attempted 'interference' with the Englishman's freedom to drink was not forgotten by the voters. When the Liberal government went to the country in 1874 it was decisively defeated. Disraeli, who had remained silent on the drink question, was swept to power. 'We have been borne down in a torrent of gin . . . ,' wrote Gladstone to his brother.

By the 1870s gin's position, role and image in society was really beginning to change. From this period onwards, it steadily became a much 'smarter' drink. The process was a slow one, for gin's past reputation could hardly have been worse. In a sense the temperance movement was partially responsible for the

change. Gin's evil reputation was maintained by its association
with the poor and the vulgar; as the poor either abstained or
turned to beer in ever-increasing numbers, gin's image improved
in the eyes of the more respectable drinker. The process was
helped by the distillers, who began to produce unsweetened or
dry gin. London dry gin was a much more subtle drink than
the old fire-water and appealed to a more sophisticated palate.

Gin was also popular with officers in the army and navy; it
figures prominently in nautical slang, for instance the 'gin pen-
nant', green and white in colour, is run up as an invitation to a
neighbouring ship. But where gin really came into its own was
in imperial India. Quinine was vital in the fight against tropical
disease and every soldier had to take a regular dose. Unfortunately it has an unpleasant bitter taste. In order to disguise
this, 'Indian tonic water' was invented. This slightly petillant
liquid was an easier and more pleasant way of drinking quinine,
but it was rather dull. Someone suggested adding spirits to it.
A variety were tried but only gin was found to combine nicely
with tonic water. The first gin and tonic had been poured.

'Pink gin' was created in a similar fashion. Naval officers,
again for medicinal reasons, were obliged to take angostura, or
'bitters' as it was called, in tropical stations. They too added gin.
They also set down the correct method of pouring a 'pink gin':
the thick angostura drops are shaken into an empty glass, which
is then revolved so that a pale brownish layer of the medicine
adheres to the inside of the glass; a quick flip of the wrist is
needed to get rid of any excess angostura, and gin can then be
added. Mixed drinks using gin had been popular before, but
these two new combinations brought a new sophistication to the
spirit.

The label 'Mother's Ruin' indicates that gin had long been
considered a drink especially favoured by women; contemporary
accounts from this period indicate that more genteel females
were not averse to a 'nip' every now and then, choosing gin
because it resembled water in appearance and left little smell

on the breath. They would take it secretly, and never refer to it by name, calling it coyly 'white wine' or, reversing the letters, 'nig'. And if *Diary of a Nobody* is to be believed, gin had also regained its reputation as a medicine. Pooter's friend Cummings declines whisky, opting for 'a little "unsweetened", as he was advised it was the most healthy spirit'. Pooter, a little behind the times, doesn't have any in the house, but 'sent Sarah round to Lockwood's for some'.

As final evidence that gin's social image was improving, examine the 1894 edition of Mrs Beeton's famous cookery book. There you will find recipes for Mint Julep and Gin Sling. Had the drink still been the devil of Hogarth's 'Gin Lane', it would hardly have qualified for inclusion in so respectable a tome.

At the same time a more dramatic revolution was taking place in the drinking habits of the whole nation. The quality of the water supply was improving, and the introduction of the railway system did much to improve the freshness of the milk on sale. More important in promoting sobriety was the development of non-intoxicating cordials like lemonade, soda water and ginger beer. The other great success of the temperance reformers was the astonishing popularity of tea. 'Every poor family is becoming a tea drinker two or three times a day,' wrote Cobden in 1864. Tea was the temperance drink and they promoted the idea of the mid-afternoon social function, in contrast to the alcoholic evening function. Cocoa too was a temperance favourite – its manufacturers, the Cadburys, Frys and Rowntrees, were prominent Quaker abstainers – and in the 1870s its consumption was increasing at a faster rate than that of tea.

The old drinking usages were also under attack. Their disappearance was perhaps inevitable as industrialization progressed but the teetotallers did much to hasten their end. The introduction of shorter working hours had decreased the need for the working man to take strong liquor to help him survive the day. And at the other end of society, port was rapidly going out of fashion – a trend begun by Prince Albert – and gout-rests were disappearing from London clubs.

Brian Harrison in *Drink and the Victorians* makes a detailed survey of statistics of drink consumption at this time. He states: 'Comparing the two five-year periods 1825-9 and 1865-9 for wine and spirits, and the years 1830-4 and 1865-9 for beer, it can be seen that *per capita* wine and beer consumption rose, and *per capita* spirits consumption fell.' But he points out that consumption of beer, wine and spirits fluctuated in relation to the general level of prosperity in the country. The more money there was available, the more people drank. Gladstone had also helped the sales of gin by creating what was known as the 'grocer's licence' in 1861. This measure enabled virtually any shopkeeper to obtain a licence to sell wines and spirits for consumption off the premises. His aim, he somewhat naïvely told the House of Commons, was to assist sobriety by placing 'wine within the reach of the lowest order of the middle classes and the better portion of the working classes'. If temperance propaganda is to be believed these worthy folk seem to have ignored the wine and invested their shillings in stocks of gin. In 1872 it was reported to the House of Commons that in Ipswich one grocer's shop sold 100 bottles of gin a week to women shoppers.

When the new century came in and the old Queen died, to be succeeded by Edward VII, a fresh, lighter atmosphere enveloped first the capital and then the country as a whole. In the bright, new Edwardian days the habit of organizing social gatherings gained momentum. The new gin-based drinks were acceptable offerings at such functions, together with sherry and sherbert. At the same time, the first American bar, the Criterion, opened in London. Here a number of exotically-named American gin-based drinks, like 'fog-cutters', could be obtained. It soon became fashionable to call in at the Criterion and taste some of these new concoctions.

The nineteenth century had ended with a constant stream of Bills intended to reform the licensing system; in 1890 twenty-five different licensing Bills were introduced, fourteen of them on a single day. All were unsuccessful.

In 1896 Lord Salisbury had appointed a Royal Commission on Licensing. It sat for three years, investigating every aspect of the drink trade. But as its members were divided between the brewing trade, the teetotal movement and 'neutrals', it rarely agreed on anything. On the now all-important issue of whether compensation should be paid to publicans who lost their licence, the Committee was hopelessly split. A majority favoured compensation, a minority of nine members were totally opposed to it. In 1904 the Conservative government introduced a new Licensing Bill, proposing compensation from a fund financed by a levy on the drink trade. This compromise appealed to Parliament and the Bill became law.

The new law was not very effective. It tended to compensate the rich brewery companies at the expense of the poor publican, and, more seriously, it failed to reduce substantially the number of pubs. In 1908 the Liberals introduced a new Bill, very similar in its provisions to Henry Bruce's ill-fated Bill of 1871, that would reduce the number of public houses by a third. It was well received by the temperance movement, but very badly by the drink trade and their supporters. A massive campaign against the Bill began, scoring a major triumph when the Liberals lost the Peckham by-election, which seems to have been fought entirely on this issue. The victorious Conservative candidate, a Mr Gooch, was hailed as 'the voice of beer!'. Ironically, he was an abstainer.

Soon the whole country was involved on one side or the other. Opponents of the Bill presented a petition bearing 600,000 signatures. By-election after by-election was lost by the Liberals. Both sides marched to Hyde Park to hear speeches and shout slogans. The issue united the temperance movement as no other ever had. The Bill progressed slowly through Parliament, hindered by nearly 1,000 tabled amendments. The Commons passed it and it lay in the hands of the Lords, solidly Conservative. The nation waited. On Friday, 27 November, 1908, they threw out the Bill. It was the end of a long struggle by the teetotallers.

Six years later war was declared on Germany. Remembering how the drinking of gin and spirits had increased during the Boer War, the government immediately brought in the Intoxicating Liquor (Temporary Restriction) Act, giving justices the power to regulate the opening hours of pubs and clubs at will. By the end of 1914 restricted hours were in operation in half the 1,000 licensing districts in England and Wales. Pubs now closed at 10 or even 9 p.m. every day of the week. There was an immediate drop in offences connected with drunkenness. For example, in the first nine months of 1914 there were 103 cases of malicious wounding in London; after the introduction of 10 p.m. closing time, the Chairman of the London Sessions, Robert Wallace, was able to announce on 1 December, 1914 : 'And, today, for almost the first time in the history of the country, there is not a single wounding case for us to deal with.'

The teetotallers rejoiced. Their glee was further increased by Lloyd George's raising of the duty on beer in his 1914 budget. But his attempt to double the duty on gin and other spirits had to be postponed indefinitely for fear of a rebellion in Ireland. Prices rose, however, from between 2d. and 4d. a tot at the outbreak of war, to 9d. or more by 1918. The teetotallers then became worried as many of their members were being perverted by army life. From July 1915 it became illegal to treat a soldier to a drink; in the same year they turned their attention to the army's rum ration, recalling how British troops had first acquired the spirit-drinking habit during Marlborough's campaigns in the Low Countries. Happily for the troops freezing in the trenches, they were not successful.

The teetotallers' chief aim, however, was total national prohibition. They hailed the Tsar, who had closed all vodka shops in military areas – 'In sternly prohibiting the sale of spirituous liquor,' commented *The Times,* 'Russia has already vanquished a greater foe than the Germans' – and the French, who had banned the sale of absinthe in many areas. When Russia was

defeated and the French were on the verge of collapse the teetotallers held up for admiration the Italian Army, which had
banned spirits. Shortly afterwards the Italian Army was routed
at Caporetto.

In May 1917 they tried a new approach. The drink trade,
'the great confederate of V.D.', was accused of being wholly
responsible for the Army's 100,000 cases of venereal disease since
1914. Unfortunately statistics showed that a high proportion of
those infected were abstainers.

Far more serious, though, was drinking on the home front,
which was said to be causing a damaging loss of production.
The Shipbuilding Employers' Federation declared that '80 per
cent of the present avoidable loss of time could be ascribed to
no other cause but drink.' Lloyd George took the matter seriously. 'We are fighting Germany, Austria and drink,' he thundered,
'and the greatest of these deadly foes is drink.' He persuaded
the King to ban all alcohol in the royal household. 'I hate doing
it, but hope it will do good,' King George noted sadly in his
diary.

In April 1915 Lloyd George introduced his Defence of the
Realm (Amendment No. 3) Bill. It proposed handing over
authority to a new Central Liquor Control Board, which could
impose any restrictions it wished, including closing pubs, limit-
ing hours and banning spirits entirely. The measure was received with rapture in Parliament; within three weeks it was
law.

The Board moved quickly to reduce opening hours. Most
places now endured the shortest licensing hours in British history,
usually from 12.30 p.m. to 2 p.m. and then from 6 p.m. to 9
p.m. Sunday hours were reduced and the 'bona fide traveller'
departed England for good. (He survived in Scotland until 1961.)
Gin could not expect to go unscathed. It didn't. Spirits for 'off'
drinking could only be sold in the afternoon and, to discourage
pocket flasks, at least a quart at a time. Their sale in railway
buffets was forbidden altogether. Perhaps worst of all, it became

compulsory to dilute spirits to below their former strength. (They have remained diluted ever since.)

D.O.R.A., as the act was known, brought about the end of an era. By 1919 shorter hours, higher prices and more civilized pubs had worked wonders. The consumption of all forms of alcohol dropped from 89 million gallons in 1914 to 37 million in 1918, and the number of cases of drunkenness in England and Wales from 184,000 to 29,000. It was also the effective end of the temperance movement. Agitation for total prohibition continued, but was never taken seriously again. Lloyd George had proved that such a drastic measure was not required. The old English virtue of common sense had prevailed.

8

The 'Noble Experiment'

For more than two hundred years, ever since genever had been
transformed from a medicine into a popular drink, one government after another had tried to curtail its manufacture and distribution. At best, these attempts were moderately but never
wholly successful; at worst, they encouraged the evils they were
intended to stamp out. In the eighteenth century the farmers
who grew the corn from which gin was distilled had always
opposed any curtailment of their main source of income. In the
nineteenth century ideas of personal liberty made the imposition
of draconian laws impossible, despite nearly seventy years of
campaigning on the part of the temperance movement. It was
not until the twentieth century that the first whole-hearted
attempt to eliminate gin altogether was made. The country
where the great battle was to be fought was not England but the
United States.

The modern temperance movement began in the United States
in about 1770, when a member of a Quaker meeting in Philadel-
phia complained that he was 'oppressed with the smell of rum
from the breaths of those who sat around him'. The first formal
pledge to abstain from spirits was taken at a meeting in New
York State in 1808, and the first pledge against all forms of intoxicating drink in Boston in 1826. The American temperance
movement thus predates the British movement by several years.

In a sense this was inevitable. From the very beginning strong liquor had a firm place in American society. The first colonists brought from Europe a taste for spirits and a faith in the healing power of *aqua vitae*. Where beer was the working man's favourite drink in England – threatened by gin on occasion as we have seen – in America it was whisky and strong spirits. The equivalent of harvest beer for the pioneers was corn whisky; it was thought to be a necessity for heavy work with the hands. The official ration for each soldier at Valley Forge in the War of Independence was a daily gill or half pint of whisky, depending on the supplies available. However, in unhappy coexistence with the pioneer's love of strong drink was his firm belief, derived from a strict, puritan religion, that drunkenness was a sin and sobriety a great virtue. Thus George Washington, who was especially fond of porter, Madeira and Port, and who distilled his own spirits, could also proclaim that drink was 'the source of all evil and the ruin of half the workmen in the country'.

In 1784 Dr Benjamin Rush published a pamphlet entitled *An Inquiry into the effects of Spirituous Liquors on the Human Body and Mind*. He advocated complete abstinence from ardent spirits, for medical reasons. Rush's writings were taken up by a preacher, Lyman Beecher, in his *Six Sermons on the Nature, Occasions, Signs, Evils and Remedy of Intemperance* (1827). Using Rush's medical arguments, Beecher brought a religious, evangelical technique into the debate. His pamphlet became in turn the ammunition of every wandering preacher.

Temperance societies were formed, and by 1834 they claimed a million members out of a population of not more than 13 million. As in England, the original movement was anti-spirits, preaching abstinence and temperance rather than prohibition. Then, in 1851, to the amazement of her neighbours, the State of Maine passed a law banning the sale of liquor throughout the state. Scenting success, the reformers doubled their attacks and within four years twelve other states had followed Maine's lead.

Though the Civil War halted the advance of the teetotallers, eleven of the states repealing their laws, with the return of peace

the urge for prohibition returned, and its advocates began to
organize. In 1869 the Prohibition Party was founded; four years
later the Women's Christian Temperance Union came into
being. Their propaganda had its roots in the eternal American
conflict between town and country. It was directed at those
Americans, the vast majority, who lived and worked on the
land, and it painted the towns and cities as decadent, evil and
wholly corrupt. In a sense the picture was a true one : certain
parts of certain cities *were* decadent, evil and corrupt. In New
York's Lower East Side in the 1870s establishments calling themselves 'distilleries' sold a potion known as 'chain lightning' for
five cents a glass; customers drank it in the luxury of the 'velvet
room' and then passed out in a semblance of comfort – a parallel
to the free straw of 'Gin Lane' London.

The saloons were also linked to criminality and, more
important, to political corruption. In return for the right to sell
liquor, the saloon-keepers delivered the votes of their districts
into the hands of the corrupt city bosses. In 1888 the St Louis
Daily Republic reported: 'The groggery, the gambling-house,
and the brothel control the city's affairs and openly boast their
power, and woe to the man who by fair deeds and respect for his
oath of office invites their enmity. He is crushed without mercy,
and a new, pliant figurehead set up in his place.' Political meetings were even held in the saloons : in 1884, out of 1,002 primary
meetings in New York City, 633 were held in saloons, and 86
in buildings immediately adjacent to saloons.

Stirred by the propaganda of the prohibitionists, Kansas
followed Maine and wrote prohibition into its constitution in
1880. A close inspection of the state of affairs in these two states
should have alerted the prohibitionists to the absurdities that
were to become so common later. For no one paid any attention
to the law. In 1910, a visitor passing through Portland, Maine,
asked a policeman if it were possible to obtain a drink. 'Do you
see that white church there?' asked the policeman. 'Well, that's
the First Methodist Church. No. You can't get a drink there,

but as far as I know, it's the *only* place in town you can't.'

Every village had a place where drink could be obtained, and in the larger towns and cities ruses that would have appealed to Captain Bradstreet were employed where necessary. Take, for instance, the 'blind pigs'.

At that time there was no law against giving liquor away as a gift. An enterprising gentleman thus bought a blind pig, established it in a comfortable box within a tented enclosure, and put out a sign : 'Look at The Blind Pig – Ten Cents a Look'. With every 'look' he gave away a drink.

It was the policy of the Prohibition Party to put up candidates for national elections, refusing to compromise with any of the established parties. Its candidates were never successful, although they did succeed in taking crucial votes from the Republicans. More effective politically was the Anti-Saloon League, founded in 1893. The League developed close links with the Republican party, and it was successful in getting candidates elected and 'dry' laws through state legislatures and Congress. The League's tactics were basic and direct : they threatened all candidates, whether for dog-catcher or President, with the loss of the 'dry' vote. Probably much of their voting strength was imaginary, but candidates were successfully blackmailed into supporting the League. While the Prohibition Party remained aloof, sticking firmly to its principles, the Anti-Saloon League threw itself into the swamp of American politics, revelling in the wheeling and dealing, the bribery and manipulation that this entailed.

Ultimately, however, it was neither the Prohibition Party nor the Anti-Saloon League that brought the issue of prohibition to the nation's attention, but a curious, deranged woman called Carry (or Carrie) Nation. Her technique was direct action : she would march into an offending saloon and smash it to pieces with a hatchet carried for this purpose. While engaged in this pursuit she would often be attacked by saloon-keepers' wives, mistresses and prostitutes. The press, of course, loved her, and her name soon became famous throughout the United States.

When she travelled to New York she was greeted uproariously
and permitted – for advertising purposes – to smash a few
saloons on the Bowery.

Carry Nation was the protoype of many of the more fanatical
prohibitionists and is worth a careful study. Born in 1846 in
Kentucky, she had the typical young Southern girl's upbringing,
with a romantic and naïve belief in love. She married the first
man to kiss her, a young doctor, who became an alcoholic. Their
daughter Charien was, as her mother wrote, '. . . peculiar. She
was the result of a drunken father and a distracted mother. The
curse of heredity is one of the most heart-breaking results of the
saloon.'

Carry's husband left her, and died shortly afterwards. She
then married the Reverend David Nation, who as well as being
a minister was also a newspaper editor and lawyer. This marriage
was no more successful than the first. They separated, and for
a while Carry Nation ran a boarding house. Her daughter's
'peculiarity' had not been caused by heredity, as Carry made
out, but more prosaically was a result of typhoid fever. The girl
eventually recovered and married, leaving her mother completely
alone. It was then that Carry joined the Women's Christian
Temperance Union, and found in the Union's violent views the
antidote to her frustrations. She herself revealed in her autobiography: 'The man I loved and married brought me bitter
grief. The child I loved so well became afflicted and never
seemed to want my love. The man I married, hoping to serve
God, I found to be opposed to all I did, as a Christian. I used
to wonder why this was. I saw others with their loving children
and husbands and I would wish their condition was mine. . . .'

It was this sad, strong mixture of frustration, religion and
hatred for alcoholism that made her stride, on 27 December,
1900, into the Carey Hotel, Wichita, where: 'The first thing
that struck me was the life-size picture of a naked woman,
opposite the mirror. . . . I called to the bartender; told him he
was insulting his own mother by having her form stripped naked

and hung up in a place where it was not even decent for a woman to be in when she had her clothes on. . . .'

Then she got down to work. Her violence even frightened her fellow temperance workers, and they tried to disown her. But she soon realized that this very violence was her strongest asset, and capitalized on it to such an extent that she even had little souvenir hatchets made which she distributed on her crusades. She appeared in *The Drunkard*, the teetotal morality play adapted from *Ten Nights in a Bar-room* by T. Arthur. She truly believed that her life had been shaped by God for this one purpose, and the disappointments of love deliberately engineered to make her His strongest preacher. The title of her autobiography, published in 1908, is revealing enough: *The Use and Need of the Life of Carry A. Nation.* No doubt Andrew Sinclair is right when he states, in *Prohibition*, that 'Her suppressed sexual desire was perverted into an itching curiosity about vice, an aggressive prurience which found its outlet in violence, exhibitionism, and self-imposed martyrdom . . .', but however misguided her motivation, and however bizarre her methods, Carry Nation probably did more than any other single American to bring home the evils of the drink trade to the American public. She made people think, even as they scoffed.

Carry Nation died of paresis, a form of muscular paralysis, in 1911, without seeing the triumph of her beliefs. By then, however, state after state was passing prohibitionist laws. By 1906 eighteen states had adopted prohibition, and in the following year Oklahoma, on its admission to the Union, went 'dry'. It was destined to remain 'dry' for the next fifty-two years, not ending prohibition until 1959.

On Saturday 16 November, 1907, the day Oklahoma went 'dry', a sad saloon-keeper in Ponca City pinned this note above his saloon door: 'Hush little saloon, don't you cry; you'll be a drug store, by and by.' Scenes similar to those at the death of Madame Geneva were witnessed that day in Oklahoma City. By eleven o'clock, 'Hades had taken a recess and was using

Broadway and Main for a playground.' By midnight the town was one huge drunken brawl. The next day 550 drinking saloons went broke.

But in this state, and in the others that had gone 'dry', the problem, as before, was that enforcement of the law was lax and often non-existent. It was easy enough to run supplies in from a neighbouring 'wet' state, or to bribe the local police officer to turn a blind eye. The reformers began to realize that only complete national prohibition would secure effective enforcement of 'dry' laws. By 1914 this had become their aim.

With the complex division of responsibility between federal (i.e. governmental) and state (i.e. local) legislation, this meant that an actual alteration of the Constitution of the United States was necessary. Such an alteration could only be made by a Constitutional Amendment, which required ratification by thirty-six of the forty-eight states. The drink trade were confident that it could never happen.

They underestimated the Anti-Saloon League. In 1914 the League began a campaign of polite terrorism over the Congress then sitting. Under its direction a flood of telegrams, letters and petitions poured in for every member seeking re-election. A body known as the Committee of Seven kept a close watch over the people's representatives in Washington. If anyone looked as though he might be wavering, the committee alerted his 'dry' constituents who then deluged him with telegrams. It was political lobbying of the utmost effectiveness.

In 1917 America entered the Great War. Swept away by patriotic fervour the people accepted numerous restrictions and impositions from above, just as the British were doing on the other side of the Atlantic. When told that they must give up drink because of the waste in cereals that should be used to feed the troops rather than to make gin and whisky, they accepted with virtuous resignation. The Food Control Act of 1917 prohibited the manufacture of distilled liquor; it was followed by a resolution submitting the Eighteenth Amendment, which would introduce complete national prohibition. Cowed by the Anti-Saloon League, by now an immensely powerful political force in Washington, Congress adopted the Amendment. On 16 January, 1919, Nebraska became the thirty-sixth state to ratify the measure; finally only two states, Rhode Island and Connecticut, refused to ratify. But an Amendment is not law until a Bill is passed in Congress making it so. It fell to a certain Mr Andrew J. Volstead, a Congressman from Minnesota, to introduce the Bill making the Eighteenth Amendment law. He lost his seat in Congress four years later for his pains.

The Volstead Act, as it became known, was chiefly written by Wayne B. Wheeler, the Anti-Saloon League's Washington attorney; Volstead was no more than a puppet. The original Bill was severe in its provisions, but these were softened as it passed through the House and the Senate. Already, under the Fourth Amendment, which prevented private citizens from being subjected to unreasonable searches of their persons and houses, and the Fifth Amendment, which not only made it impossible for people to give evidence against themselves but prevented them from being tried twice for the same offence, the Amendment was something of a dead letter, impossible to enforce. The Senate weakened it further by permitting people to possess liquor in their homes and hotels, and to consume it there.

Ultimately the Volstead Act made it a crime to manufacture or sell any beverage containing more than 0.5 per cent alcohol. (The weakest alcoholic drink is about 2.5 per cent alcohol.) It set the maximum penalty for a first conviction at imprisonment for six months and a fine of $1,000. *But it was not a criminal offence to buy drink.*

It seems incredible today that anyone supposed such a law was worth passing; even more incredible is the machinery which the authorities set up in order to enforce the law. Responsibility was lodged with the Bureau of Internal Revenue, through a Prohibition Unit headed by the Federal Commissioner of Prohibition. Under his command were 1,500 Prohibition agents.

1,500! The population of the United States was then 125 million, thus there was one agent to more than 83,000 citizens, or geographically, one agent to each 2,340 square miles.

President Wilson vetoed the Volstead Act in 1919, but Congress and the Senate passed it over his veto. The date was set: 16 January, 1920, and it seems that the vast majority of Americans seriously believed that drink would simply disappear on that day and that American children would grow up to ask: 'Daddy, what *was* gin?'. A minority – the naïve drinkers – simply didn't understand what was happening, and were thus most surprised on that January morning when they found the saloons selling soda-pop and the liquor stores shut down. The honour of being the first person arrested under the Volstead Act went to one Giovanni Volpe, a wine merchant in Greenwich Village. Knowing no English he was entirely ignorant of the new law and he supposed that the officer who arrested him at 1.45 a.m. was charging him with violation of the saloon-closing law.

There was another minority, however, who had read the law, even down to the smallest print, and who were fully prepared on that January morning. Among their number were the rich, who laid down vast stocks of liquor – the Yale Club bought enough to last its members fourteen years – because they had noted that it was not illegal to supply drink that had been purchased before the Act came into force; the owners of the speakeasies that soon opened up all over America; and the illicit distillers. The latter – there were thousands of them hidden in the Appalachian Mountains alone – decided to lie low for a while to see how things went. They had been doing a brisk trade before the Act, but feared that the government was now going to take more interest in their operations.

On the last night of legal drinking there were mock funerals held in New York, reminiscent of the processions in London in 1736, and ladies at Reinsenweber's bar were presented with compacts in the form of coffins. The revivalist Billy Sunday held

a joyful funeral, burying a twenty-foot effigy of John Barley-
corn, and hundreds of other 'drys' celebrated the death of the
demon drink. Their triumphant rejoicings were a little
premature.

At first things seemed to go well for the prohibitionists. The
drinkers were still using up their stocks. The agents swung into
action. New York thrilled to the exploits of 'Izzy' and 'Moe'
who adopted a variety of bizarre disguises as they went about
their work. In general, however, these enforcement agents were
not very impressive. Many were dismissed police officers, some
had criminal records, but most ominous of all for the future of
prohibition was the paucity of their salaries. The average agent
received less than $2,000 a year. There were hundreds of shady
gentlemen in New York, Chicago or Los Angeles who were
prepared to pay them that amount for looking the other way for
an hour.

By 1922 private stocks of liquor were running out and America
entered the second stage of the prohibition era – the Home Brew
age. Chemistry became the new national craze and it was soon
discovered that almost every living plant in the land could form
the basis of an alcoholic drink. The resulting brews varied in
effect : from hysteria to coma to sudden death. The 'professional'
illicit distillers, those who had been making 'moonshine' for
years, came into their own, pumping out gallons of illegal alcohol
for distribution by 'bootleggers'.

The bootlegger, although depicted in popular fiction as a
smuggler, was in most cases only a middleman or agent. Respectable people would talk of 'my bootlegger' just as they would
refer to 'my butcher' or 'my hairdresser'. He obtained his stocks
in a variety of ways. Huge amounts of liquor were 'imported'
from Canada, and from the West Indies – the official 'low
estimate' was 40 million dollars' worth a year. The other source
of properly-made spirits was the government warehouses : in
1920 there were 50,550,498 gallons of whisky under bond, by
1933 stocks had shrunk mysteriously to 18,442,955 gallons.

Industrial alcohol, permitted under the Volstead Act for medicinal and other vital purposes, was 'diverted'. Official estimates
in 1926 put the amount of industrial alcohol diverted to the
bootleggers at between 50 and 60 million gallons a year. Since
each gallon of industrial alcohol was transformed into three
gallons of so-called gin or whisky, the volume of and profits
from the trade were considerable. The Prohibition Bureau tried
to halt the trade by adding poisons to the industrial alcohol, but
the bootleggers and their customers were not deterred, even
when the number of deaths from drinking this poison began to
increase alarmingly. The famous 'bathtub gin' was made by
mixing industrial alcohol with glycerine and oil of juniper. It
was served with ginger ale to hide the flavour, but the after-
effects remained horrendous. The bootlegger's final principal
source was the illicit distiller. He prospered for a while, but then
large criminal distributors began to move in and proceeded to
rationalize the trade by setting up large, professionally-run
distilleries to cater for the growing demand.

Bootlegging had become the most profitable industry in the
United States. The small man made his fortune :

> Mother makes brandy from cherries;
> Pop distils whisky and gin;
> Sister sells wine from the grapes on our vine –
> Good grief how the money rolls in !

while the big men – Capone, Diamond *et al.* – squabbled and
murdered for millions. Chester LaMare, who ran Detroit's
underworld, was estimated to be grossing $215,000,000 a year
from bootlegging in 1928. Malvern Hall Tillitt, an eminent
statistician, estimated at the height of prohibition that the citizens of the United States were paying annually $4,414,000,000
for their illicit liquor. It was not surprising that men were
prepared to kill for a piece of this market.

The prohibitionists had given birth to a monster, but

characteristically they refused to admit it. Instead they pressed
for harsher penalties. Enforcement was impossible – New York
had less than 200 agents and an estimated 32,000 speakeasies –
and the people knew it. Prohibition had the effect of bringing
the whole of the law into disrepute, and of creating an organized
criminal underworld that has survived and flourished ever since.
The police in many areas had soon given up all hope of enforcing
the law, leaving it to the dwindling band of uncorrupted prohibition agents. What had begun as a 'noble experiment' was
tearing America apart.

From time to time, American prohibitionists would try to
extend their dry grip on lands across the sea. Britain, perhaps
because the language was the same, was a favourite stamping
ground for these evangelists. Most famous was probably W. E.
'Pussyfoot' Johnson, an intrepid gospeller who was invited over
by the United Kingdom Alliance. He got his nickname because
of his stealthy work in tracking down illicit drink in the States.

His reception in the United Kingdom was, however, far
from friendly. While taking part in a debate at Essex Hall in
London, 'Pussyfoot' was kidnapped by medical students from
King's College, who invaded the hall, armed with bags of flour
and stink bombs. He was paraded through the streets by students
chanting :

> Mr Pussyfoot, miaow-wow !
> Mr Pussyfoot, miaow-wow !
> Fancy coming from America to try
> To make old England dry !
>
> Uncle Sam stood it like a lamb,
> But if you think we are going to allow
> Any crank of a Yank to put us in the water tank –
> Mr Pussyfoot, miaow-wow !

When rescued by the police, Mr Pussyfoot declared that he

had 'had a good time'; and although he later lost the sight of one eye as a result of a stone thrown during the students' 'rag', he still remained cheerful and defiant. He made a gramophone record called *What I See with My Blind Eye* in which he described the 'dry' world of the future. The world is still waiting for Mr Pussyfoot's vision to come about.

9

The Cocktail Age

Curiously, it was from 1920 onwards that the cocktail, a new social phenomenon, grew steadily in popularity. Some of this growth, at least in the United States, can be put down to the low standard of much of the illicit gin. Poisonous lead and zinc from unclean stills often found their way into the final product. As in eighteenth-century Britain, all kinds of ingredients were added to the distilled liquid to give it, or to disguise, its taste. Yet this does not explain why the cocktail should have become so popular even in countries where there was no form of prohibition and where good gin could be obtained in any quantity.

There was nothing particularly original about a cocktail. The habit of mixing drinks in order to produce a new drink has existed as long as alcohol has been consumed. Toddy, for example, a mixture of strong spirits, boiling water, sugar, lemon and spices, was a favourite beverage long before gin was invented. But it was only when unsweetened gin came onto the market that the making up of new drinks became more widespread, for it was soon discovered that unsweetened gin, unlike any other alcohol, blended ideally with all kinds of ingredients, to produce a whole new range of drinks.

To most people, the cocktail is a short, sharp, rather strong drink which usually, but not always, has a gin basis. There are almost as many theories to explain the origin of its name as there are different cocktails.

The oldest, and possibly the most likely theory is that the word 'cocktail' was a distortion of the French word *coquetel,* which was a mixed wine-cup, made for centuries at Bordeaux. When Lafayette's French officers joined the American Revolutionary Army in 1779, they brought the word with them to describe any kind of mixed drink.

Later, when cocktails became well established, historians of American folk-lore searched back in United States history to see where it originated; and, though placing the date of its first use correctly around 1779, did not wish the word to have a foreign, even a friendly foreign, beginning. Therefore they invented or improved on a number of local legends.

One of the most popular of these was the legend of Betsy Flanagan. She was reputed to have been the widow of an American Revolutionary soldier killed in action against the British. She ran a tavern near Yorktown which was much frequented by the French officers serving in Washington's army. Nearby lived an American Tory loyalist, for not every American supported the Revolution. This particular loyalist had a very fine chicken run, far superior to anything owned by his Republican neighbours, including Betsy Flanagan. This so annoyed Betsy that she stole her neighbour's chickens, and served them up for dinner to her French military customers. As an added gesture, she decorated the French officers' glasses with the tail feathers of the unfortunate roosters. The drinks were 'bracers', a special mixture of different drinks which she always prepared for them. On seeing the novel decoration, one of the French officers lifted his glass to her and said, *'Vive le* Cock-tail'. After that the officers always referred to their mixed bracers as cocktails.

A further legend, rather more romantic but equally unreliable, is centred around another innkeeper of about the same period, but this time a man. He was mad-keen on cock-fighting, and had a splendid bird called Washington. Just before an important cock-fight, Washington mysteriously disappeared. The innkeeper

7 The ingredients of gin. *Top:* juniper berries; *bottom, left to right:* angelica root, orris root and powder, coriander seeds.

8 The Eagle Tavern, one of the most ostentatious of the Victorian gin palaces.

9 A pawn shop in Bethnal Green.

was in despair and, in true Hans Andersen style, offered the hand
of his beautiful daughter, Bessie, to any man who brought the
precious bird back.

Within an hour, an impoverished American soldier who had
been courting Bessie against the innkeeper's wishes, providen-
tially turned up with the missing bird. Whether the innkeeper
suspected that he had been the victim of a wily plot on the part
of his daughter and her lover is not recorded. He was so pleased
to get his champion bird back that he readily agreed to the
marriage.

During the excitement of the subsequent engagement festivi-
ties, Bessie, who served as barmaid, got her bottles all mixed
up, and served her customers an extraordinary mixture, which
turned out, much to everyone's surprise, to be rather good. The
new drinks were named 'cocktails' in honour of the plumage of
her father's newly restored fighter.

The legend of a girl mixing drinks in a moment of stress
occurs over and over again. The most popular one is usually
set in one of those decayed 'Deep South' homes. Here, the girl,
usually in her teens or just married, is set to make the much-
loved mint juleps. In her ignorance and confusion she mixes
the wrong drinks. Her guests, either out of kindness or from
genuine conviction, tell her that the drinks are wonderful, and as
brilliant as the mixed colours found in a cock's tail.

Other theories are even more far-fetched : a successful gam-
bler on a Mississippi show-boat would make up a concoction
from all the bottles in the bar, and mix it up with a stirrer that
looked like a cock's tail. Another told how American naval
officers on visiting Mexico were served drinks by a beautiful
girl called Xoctl (pronounced, as some newspapers today would
helpfully explain to their readers, cocktail), and the drink, a
mixed one, was named in her honour. A further legend says that
it was British naval officers who visited Mexico, and there was
not a beautiful girl but a popular barman who used a root
called a *cola de galo,* (translated as a 'cocktail') to stir his mixed

drinks instead of the usual wooden spoon. Non-thoroughbred horses used to be called 'cock-tailed' horses because their tails were 'cocked' [i.e. plaited] to indicate their mixed breeding. Drinks with mixed ingredients were, by derivation, known as 'cock-tailed' drinks.

Finally, in eighteenth-century Britain, cock-ale, a mixture of spirits, was given to fighting cocks while they were training; and after a fight, the owners of a victorious bird would count the number of feathers the exhausted cock still had in his tail, and a beverage with this number of drinks mixed into it was immediately consumed. A mighty cocktail indeed.

The word may perhaps have originated, like so many new inventions, more or less simultaneously in different parts of the world. Whatever its origin, and you can take your choice, it was in current use by the beginning of the nineteenth century. It is mentioned in an American magazine called *The Balance* in 1806 and is described as any drink where bitters was added to a mixture of alcohol. The famous cocktail word 'sling' also appears in the same magazine, for the author notes that the resultant concoction is known as a 'bittered sling'.

Jerry Thomas, a barman in New York and San Francisco, published a book in the mid-nineteenth century called *The Bon Vivant's Guide, or How to Mix Drinks*. As he spent a good deal of time in 1859 travelling around Europe looking for new recipes, it is probable that he introduced many of the new mixed drinks to the countries he visited. The most receptive of these was undoubtedly the British Isles, where diversity of drinks has always been evident.

At this time, cocktails were usually drunk on picnics or at race-meetings, rarely indoors, and certainly never at receptions or parties. Sometimes, the old medical qualities of gin were remembered and a cocktail was considered a good tonic for those who were 'poorly'.

Jerry Thomas was a dedicated man. He travelled everywhere with his own mixing equipment of glasses, silver spoons and

An American bartender

dishes, said to be worth £1,000. He mixed his drinks in large open beakers, and was the first to stick a slice of lemon on the side of the glass. He spent years searching for the perfect flavouring, particularly bitters, with which to give a special taste to his *Fancy Gin.*

In 1882, Harry Johnson published in New York his *Bartenders' Manual, or How to Mix Drinks of the Present Style.* This was a complete guide to the many American cocktails that were becoming popular in American-style bars all over the world.

These early cocktails had all sorts of recondite names such as *Daisy, Shrub, Crusta* and *Smash.* Most of these names were of a transient nature. They would be popular slang for a few years – one can visualize Lupin shocking his father, poor old Charles Pooter, in the *Diary of a Nobody,* with one of these new slangy

names – and then disappear. Only a very select few have survived.

It is unlikely that the grim, unsmiling and humourless prohibitionists realized that by introducing total abstinence to the
United States, they were, among other things, going to give the
cocktail a tremendous fillip. Some, if not most, of the 'bathtub
gin' produced by the 'stills behind the hills' was so awful that
it could only be drunk heavily disguised. The moonshiners had
already tried to disguise the raw alcoholic taste by including
such interesting ingredients as dead rats, offal, methylated spirits
and vitriol when preparing their mash. Some of the resultant
concoctions were deadly, but even those that were not needed
careful disguising. The answer was the cocktail. So the Cocktail
Age began in 1920.

During the first decade of prohibition, the speakeasies thrived
on the cocktail's popularity. America was enjoying a boom and
people were prepared to pay anything for drinks. The average
pre-prohibition saloon served its drinks straight, and mixed drinks
were considered effeminate. Prohibition ended this by providing
liquor that could not be drunk straight, and by encouraging
women to enter the drinking-places for the first time.

The depression of 1930 hit the speakeasies hard. People were
reluctant to abandon their new-found appetite for cocktails, but
they were unable to pay exorbitant prices and willing to forgo
the luxury and delicious furtiveness of the speakeasy in order to
obtain their drink. The situation produced a new method of
retailing liquor : the 'cordial shop'. These were tiny little shops,
gaudily decorated, with shelves in their windows filled with non-
alcoholic, 'Old World' liqueurs. Their speciality was the sale of
'dollar gin' in twenty-six-ounce bottles, labelled 'Gordon's' or
'London Dry' or with the name of some other famous brand.
The bootleggers had special printing presses set up to produce
counterfeit labels, and bottling plants to imitate distinctive bottles.

'Dollar gin' flooded New York, nearly ruining the speakeasy
trade overnight. The cordial shops were accessible, day or night,

they would deliver, and their drink was comparatively cheap. By 1931 the gin had dropped to 75 cents a bottle; a cocktail in a speakeasy cost from 60 cents to $2.50 a glass. When the cordial shops appeared the speakeasies were forced to reduce their prices. They also put an end to 'bathtub gin'. It was cheaper to buy one's poison ready-made.

In England, happily, the dedicated cocktail drinker did not have to brave the forces of law and order before he could enjoy his favourite mixed drink. He could obtain it at a bar, or at a new form of social function that had arrived on the heels of the cocktail fad : the cocktail party.

By the 1920s, the symmetrical orderliness of the English afternoon, with tea between 4 and 4.30 p.m., was being increasingly threatened. In the aftermath of the Great War many of the old rules and taboos of polite society had become oppressive and unnecessary. Among them was the practice of dressing elaborately for dinner. Under the new order, one still dressed up, but the clothes became much simpler and less ritualistic and therefore required less time to put on. It was no longer necessary to spend two hours every evening dressing. This was welcomed by most people, but what *did* one do between six and eight?

The answer came from America : one gave a cocktail party. According to Lord Kinross in his book on Booth's the distillers, *The Kindred Spirit,* the cocktail party was introduced to London by an American-born hostess named Madame Alfredo de Pena in the late 'twenties. However, Alec Waugh in *Merchants of Wine* (curiously, a history of Gilbey's, Booth's great rivals) recalls how in 1924 he discussed with the painter C. R. W. Nevinson and his wife the difficulty of finding anything to do in London between tea and dinner. The Nevinsons thought it would be a good idea to hold a party at that time, and to serve cocktails. Thirty invitations were dispatched, but only two guests turned up. The idea of going to a party at six o'clock was still alarming enough to scare off most of those invited. When Waugh gave a party himself a year later he took the precaution of inviting his friends to tea at half-past four and not starting to serve cocktails until half-past five.

Whoever gave London its first cocktail party, and when, it is indisputable that by the end of the decade this new function was the rage of high society. It was particularly taken up by the 'Bright Young Things' who, although few in number, set the tone of the whole era. Feverishly busy doing almost nothing, the Bright Young Things were a product of the appalling war that had killed so many men. They were trying somehow to make up for all the misery that had been endured so stoically during the four years between 1914-1918. Many were young widows trying desperately, in new emotions, to forget their despair; most were wealthy, or came from a background where luxury was a daily necessity.

That there were at the same time millions of unemployed, and that many millions more existed on near starvation wages, only increased their desire to live frenetically for the moment. In the novels of Evelyn Waugh, from *Decline and Fall* to *Vile Bodies*, one can find a faithful picture of the brittle, comic and yet infinitely sad world of the Bright Young Things and of their particular period, the Cocktail Age.

10

Seven Thousand Varieties

As the cocktail craze swept the world during the 1920s and '30s, everyone was giving parties and experimenting with new mixtures. And there was certainly room for experimentation. H. L. Mencken, while researching the etymology of the word 'cocktail' for his *American Language,* hired a mathematician to calculate how many different cocktails could be mixed from the stock of a first-class bar. The answer was 17,864,392,788.

In reality, of course, no one ever made even a millionth of that number. John Doxat, author of *Drinks and Drinking,* estimates that about 7,000 different cocktails were being made at the height of the Cocktail Age, a figure confirmed by the United Kingdom Bartenders' Guild. The great majority of these mixtures had a gin basis.

The father of all cocktails and the most durable is undoubtedly the Martini. Accounts of its origin are typically confused. Mencken traced the word back to 1899 and derived it from Martini & Rossi, the makers of vermouth. Others prefer the legend that it was invented by a Signor Martini, barman at the Knickerbocker Hotel, in about 1910. Then there are those who agree with this date, but say that the barman's name was Martinez and the hotel was the Waldorf Astoria. . . .

Similar disagreement reigns over the important question of how a Martini is made. There seems to be general agreement that its constituents are gin and French vermouth, but no con-

sensus as to the correct proportions of each ingredient or to the
way they are mixed. The Martini & Rossi Company recommend
a ratio of three gins to one vermouth, mixed together with ice.
A squeeze of lemon peel should be added to the glass. But the
lover of a 'real' Martini will reply that excellent as this drink
may be it is not a dry Martini in the true sense. Doxat claims
that the proportions should never be less than seven gins to one
vermouth, and that ideally it should be eleven-twelfths gin to
one-twelfth vermouth, that at least two fluid ounces of gin should
be used, and that nothing else should be added. This Martini
would be dry, but not as dry as the result of this recipe: 'Drink
a little vermouth. Exhale into the interior of a cocktail glass and
then fill it with gin.' Or, indeed, as dry as the Martini made by
a famous barman who declared that only the *shadow* of the
vermouth bottle should fall across the gin!

Obviously, it is a case of experimenting until one finds the
perfect blend to suit one's own taste and then sticking to it,
oblivious of the criticism and derision of fellow 'experts'. Mixing
a Martini is not a mundane, everyday affair, to be performed
automatically, but a religious rite, a never-ending quest for perfection, to be undertaken in a spirit of reverence and with complete concentration.

Take the case of Eric X. In his youth Eric had been a Bright
Young Thing, determined to enjoy himself now because 'nothing
would last'. Each of the Bright Young Things wanted to achieve
some tiny personal perfection that was, in itself, pointless. Some
would drive their Bentleys round and round Sloane Square in
pursuit of the lap record (Margot Metroland in Evelyn Waugh's
Scoop drives her Baby Austin down the entrance of the ladies'
lavatory there), others would stand motionless on their hands in
the middle of cocktail parties. Eric aspired to be known as the
maker of the perfect Martini.

No hectic thrusting together, high above the head, of ice,
gin and vermouth in a cheap-looking silver shaker for him. He
approached each evening's task with the care and devotion of a

priest preparing the sacrament. First, there was the question of the temperature of the room. It had to be just right, not too hot, not too cold. Then there were the ice cubes. They had to be made from fresh spring water, not polluted tap water. He had his favourite gin, his favourite vermouth.

He would lay a clean, white cloth on a glass-topped table (this, for some reason, was also essential), place his glass mixers, spoons and bottles in their correct places, and make sure that the slop basin for failures was in position on the floor.

Then, with excruciating slowness, Eric would pour out the ingredients into the mixing glass, stir, mix, and pour out *'une goutte'* with a tasting glass. If the mixture was not satisfactory he would dispose of it ruthlessly, clean all his instruments, collect himself and start again.

When, eventually, he had produced what he considered a proper dry Martini, he would go over to his wife, who by then had changed for dinner and was standing by the fireplace, and offer it to her with a modest and self-depreciatory :

'Not my finest, but acceptable, I hope, all the same.'

This was Eric's method, special to him. Other experts would find his Martinis undrinkable : too much vermouth . . . too little gin . . . ice in *cubes,* would you believe? Some connoisseurs are adamant that a touch of bitters is necessary, added to the glass, not to the drink. Some, iconoclastic Americans at that, declare that vermouth is unnecessary, and that gin should be drunk 'on the rocks' (mixed neat with ice in a large glass), but then that is not a cocktail but a snifterini. Others maintain that ice inside the drink weakens the Martini; the ice should therefore be packed around the mixing glass, or the prepared concoction left in the fridge. Ready-made Martinis are available in bottles, but no gentleman would be seen drinking one.

The invention of new cocktails was the speciality of barmen and it invested their profession with more respectability and charisma than ever before. There was, and still is, in Paris a famous bar called *Harry's.* Situated at cinq rue Daunou, it was known to all visitors in the 'thirties as 'sank roo doe noo'. The barman called himself Harry, but was evidently not the Harry who had first brought his bar over from New York in 1911. Here, at around 11 o'clock in the morning, the more cosmopolitan citizens of Paris and the expatriate Americans who had set up there would gather to drink their first Martinis of the day (always made with Noilly Prat vermouth) or one of the many other cocktails available there.

It was here that the *Sidecar* (equal proportions of gin and brandy, plus lemon and ice) had been invented. Another of Harry's inventions was the famous *White Lady*. This consisted of gin and cointreau, in the proportions of two gins to one cointreau and one lemon juice. The special ingredient was a small quantity of white of egg, giving the concoction a whitish, slightly opaque look, not unlike a woman's white satin evening dress. The *White Lady* was honoured in verse :

> Where ties are white and women wear
> As little as they frankly dare
> White ladies are in great demand
> (But in a glass you understand).

In London there were famous barmen at the Savoy, Quaglino's, Oddenino's, Crockford's, Ciro's, the Carlton, the Café de Paris, the Berkeley Buttery and many other clubs, casinos and hotels. Two of these pre-war barmen are still with us : Eddie Clarke, who started at the London Casino, then opened his own bar, Eddie's Albemarle Club, and now lives in retirement in Tenerife; and Laurie Ross, originally at the Carlton, until recently still dispensing drinks, particularly his speciality the *Rickey,* in the downstairs bar of the Ritz Hotel.

At lunchtime cocktails were consumed in the bars of restaurants and hotels, in the evening the casinos and nightclubs came into their own. Typical of the pre-war nightclubs was Casani's. Here, in quiet and unostentatious surroundings, one could listen to Charlie Kunz ('Clap hands, here comes Charlie') at the piano, or dance until the early hours of the morning, with nothing more to drink than one or two White Ladies. Bacon and eggs, that ritualistic nightclub breakfast, costing about two shillings and sixpence a head, would be served around three in the morning. Casani himself, a small man with a wooden ear which he would sometimes unscrew and leave on a table, would sit and chat from time to time with his guests. The atmosphere was curiously innocent, resembling a private and rather exclusive party given to friends. And in a way, this is what it was, for the drink regulations then in force made it illegal to sell alcohol after closing hours except in 'private' houses and then only if one was drinking one's own bottle. There was, on joining, a strange rigmarole of signing for dozens of bottles of every kind of drink. In some clubs the head waiter would mark the bottle and produce it again when the member next appeared.

As with all the greatest crazes, the cocktail was responsible for a mass of peripheral gadgetry and handiwork. Couturiers and dress shops produced cocktail dresses, usually short and of simple design, specifically tailored for cocktail parties. The novelty manufacturers deluged the market with cocktail shakers, glasses, swizzle sticks, and decorated sticks for transfixing the olives, maraschino cherries, angelica peel and slices of lemon that were so essential to the final appearance of the perfect cocktail. Stationers stocked garish cocktail mats, and designed special cocktail party invitations. Furniture manufacturers produced Art Deco cocktail cabinets, with gleaming steel and glass interiors and shelves and drawers cunningly designed to hold all the paraphernalia that one needed to produce the evening's drink. Finally, there were the books, hundreds of them, which attempted to initiate the layman, the poor fellow who could never afford even one White Lady in Quaglino's (or indeed would never have been allowed into the bar) into the mysteries of making and appreciating good cocktails.

Cocktails had been given fanciful names from the begin-

ning, and the authors of these books evidently spent many hours
thinking up new ones with which to christen their new concoctions. But somehow they could never equal the sheer power of
the original American names – *Connecticut Eye-opener, Ala-
bama Fog-cutter, Lightning Smash, Thunderbolt Cocktail,* or
even the more prosaic *Bronx* – which seem to reflect the dubious
and often deadly nature of their original constituents.

The celebrities of the time from the theatrical, sporting and
social worlds were approached to give their names to new cocktails. An interesting little booklet entitled *An Anthology of Cocktails, together with Selected Observations by a distinguished
gathering, and diverse Thoughts for Great Occasions* was published by Booth's. It consisted of a photograph of the 'personality',
as he or she would now be called, with the selected cocktail, his
or her comment and the 'Thought for the Occasion'.

Thus that popular matinée idol and composer of light music,
Ivor Novello, was accorded a cocktail called Star Cocktail. It
consisted of an equal mixture of gin and calvados, with a dash of
French vermouth, Italian vermouth and grapefruit juice.

Other theatrical people in the booklet were Sybil Thorndike,
whose thought for the occasion was the cryptic 'The acting of
women prompts the action of men'; Yvonne Arnaud ($\frac{1}{3}$ gin,
$\frac{1}{3}$ vermouth, $\frac{1}{3}$ cassis), who made a play on her name with 'Ah
yes!' to the firm's product and 'Arnaud' to all others; Basil
Dean, the film producer, whose proposed cocktail sounds rather
sickly, a mixture of gin, maraschino, lemon juice and raspberry
syrup; and Tom Walls, the comedian and racehorse owner, who
was featured with two of his horses, and whose thought for
the occasion was 'Laugh and the world laughs with you – drink
and it does the same'.

The popularity of these drinks usually lasted only as long as
their namesakes', being outstripped by those named after more
humble men, barmen and waiters at the famous clubs and restaurants. The original John Collins, for instance, was head waiter
at Limmer's in Conduit Street. The drink that bears his name

is made as follows : Squeeze the juice of a lemon into a tall glass, add a heaped teaspoonful of sugar, large jigger (2 ounces or so) of gin, plenty of ice and fill the glass with soda water. Experts recommend that one stirs the glass between each gulp, to make sure that the sugar is well mixed and the drink is effervescing. Some people also add a dash of bitters.

The *John Collins* is not a cocktail but a 'gin sling', so called because it should be slung down the throat. The *Gimlet,* however, is a cocktail, as well as having the reputation of being the 'mainstay of the British Empire'. It is made by pouring 3 parts of dry gin and 1 part of Rose's lime juice into a shaker, adding ice, and shaking vigorously.

The theatre, too, siezed upon the cocktail party as a suitable background for the dramas and comedies then being enacted; it soon became one of the clichés of the West End stage.

Frederick Lonsdale was the first to use the cocktail as an appendage to the action of a play. In *Spring Cleaning,* produced at the St Martin's Theatre, London, on 29 February, 1925, a young society girl, Fay Collen, when asked how she feels, replies : 'Whacked to the world, darling. Ten to five this morning when I got home; up at half-past nine, at it all day. Heavens, what a life ! Margaret darling, a cocktail with a dash of absinthe in it !'

Fay is a genuine representative of the Cocktail Age. A little later she describes a party she has attended: 'Willie turned Jacques out of his own bar and mixed the cocktails himself. What he put in them, the Lord alone knows. All I know is, they affected poor Jane so much we all became hysterical. . . .'

Lonsdale perhaps became a little carried away by his cocktail motif. Whenever any new character arrives on stage he is immediately given a cocktail from the cocktail table which is a permanent fixture of Richard Sones's drawing room, the setting for Acts One and Three of *Spring Cleaning.* Those already on stage are continuously pouring out cocktails for themselves and others. Life in 1925 was a thirst-making business.

Others were to follow Lonsdale's lead, notably Noel Coward

who featured cocktails in *The Vortex* and *Fallen Angels* and raised this genre to the level of an art. But it was left to T. S. Eliot to take the drawing-room comedy, cocktails and all, into the realms of literature. His tragi-comedy *The Cocktail Party* was first performed in 1949.

One of the characters, Julia Shuttlethwaite, has this to say about cocktail parties:

> The only reason for a cocktail party
> For a gluttonous old woman like me
> Is a really nice tit-bit. I can drink at home.
> Edward, give me another of those delicious olives.
> What's that? Potato crisps? No, I can't endure them.

Perhaps there was more to a cocktail party than this, but these five lines do somehow seem to sum up the feeling of such an event.

For those readers who are tempted to try some of the once famous cocktails, there follows a brief list of recipes. Cocktail utensils may be hard to find today, but if possible the following should be obtained: a $\frac{1}{2}$ gill, a $\frac{1}{4}$ gill, a 1/5 gill and a $\frac{1}{6}$ gill measure; a mixing glass and mixing spoon; a cocktail shaker; and a strainer. Robert, 'well known as an expert, first at the Royal Automobile Club, then the Criterion, finally at the Embassy Club', from whose book *Cocktails: How to Mix Them* these recipes are taken, recommends that the 'gentleman mixer' should also keep on his sideboard: A bottle of dry gin 'of superior quality', a bottle of matured Scotch whisky, a bottle of good cognac brandy, a bottle of pale sherry, a bottle each of French and Italian vermouth, a small bottle of Angostura bitters, a small bottle of orange bitters, a bottle of plain sugar syrup, a bottle of orange syrup and a bottle of grenadine or raspberry syrup.

BLOODHOUND COCKTAIL

Fill the shaker half full of broken ice and add :
6 nice raspberries
½ teaspoonful of maraschino
⅙ gill of dry gin.
⅙ gill of French vermouth.
⅙ gill of Italian vermouth.
Shake well and strain into a cocktail glass, taking care that
the pips do not pass through the strainer into the glass.

BRONX

Fill the shaker half full of broken ice and add :
The juice of a quarter of an orange.
⅙ gill of dry gin.
⅙ gill of French vermouth.
⅙ gill of Italian vermouth.
Shake well and strain into a cocktail glass. A dash of orange
bitters can also be added.
This cocktail is named after the well-known New York zoo.

DEMPSEY COCKTAIL

Fill the shaker half full of broken ice and add :
2 dashes of absinthe.
1 teaspoonful of grenadine.
⅙ gill of gin.
⅓ gill of calvados.
Shake well and strain into a cocktail glass.
This drink was introduced at Deauville in 1921, after Dempsey's victory over Carpentier.

GLOOM RAISER

A cocktail invented by Robert himself at the R.A.C. Club in
1915. The ingredients, which should be stirred, are :
$\frac{1}{3}$ gill of Gordon's dry gin.
$\frac{1}{6}$ gill of Noilly Prat vermouth.
2 dashes of grenadine.
2 dashes of absinthe.
Squeeze lemon-peel on top.

H.P.W. COCKTAIL

A cocktail invented by the celebrated bar-tender 'Charlie' of
the Racket Club in New York, as a compliment to the prominent millionaire member of the Club, Mr Harry Payne
Whitney.
$\frac{1}{6}$ gill of gin.
$\frac{1}{3}$ gill of Italian vermouth.
1 slice of an orange.
Shake well and strain into a cocktail glass.

MONKEY'S GLAND COCKTAIL

Fill the shaker half full of broken ice and add :
2 teaspoonfuls of absinthe.
2 teaspoonfuls of grenadine.
$\frac{1}{4}$ gill of gin.
$\frac{1}{4}$ gill of fresh orange juice.
Shake well and strain into a cocktail glass.
Robert tells us that this cocktail is the invention of Harry
MacElhone, the barman at Ciro's Club, and that it was 'very
popular in Deauville and London'. He makes no mention of
where it got its curious name.

PRINCESS MARY

Another of Harry's inventions. He introduced it in honour of Princess Mary's wedding to Lord Lascelles in February 1922.
Fill the shaker half full of broken ice and add :
$\frac{1}{6}$ gill of dry gin.
$\frac{1}{6}$ gill of Crème-de-Cacao.
$\frac{1}{6}$ gill of fresh cream.
Shake well and strain into a cocktail glass.

SILVER STREAK

Fill the shaker half full of broken ice and add :
$\frac{1}{4}$ gill of Kümmel.
$\frac{1}{4}$ gill of dry gin.
Shake well and strain into a cocktail glass.

YELLOW RATTLER COCKTAIL

A 'cowboy's cocktail'. Fill the shaker half full of broken ice and add :
1 dash of orange bitters.
$\frac{1}{6}$ gill of Martini & Rossi vermouth.
$\frac{1}{3}$ gill of dry gin.
A small bruised white onion.
Shake well and strain into a cocktail glass.

Finally, for the morning after, here is Robert's recipe for a *Gin Fizz* :
Fill the shaker half full of broken ice and add :
A teaspoonful of sugar syrup.
The juice of one lemon.
$\frac{3}{4}$ gill of gin.
Shake well, strain into a tumbler and fill up with cold soda water. Drink immediately.

'No More Money in the Bank'

> Got no money in the bank;
> What's to do about it?
> Let's put out the lights,
> And go to sleep.

As is so often the case, it was a popular song that captured the spirit of a particular time. In this case it is the 1930s, a time of world-wide economic depression and of growing fascist ascendancy in Europe.

In America, by 1930, enforcement of the Eighteenth Amendment was impossible. Americans everywhere were breaking the law with impunity, and the police, who had never had much enthusiasm for prohibition, had given up trying to enforce it. But despite the free access to liquor now enjoyed by the drinking population, the American public was beginning to sicken of the whole business. Millionaire gangsters were amusing, even admirable, in the heady, prosperous days of the 'twenties, but in the depressed, despairing days of the early 'thirties their wealth and lawlessness came to be resented. America began to count the cost of her ten-year spree, particularly in respect of the nation's youth.

Determined agitation against prohibition started to be heard for the first time. The Association Against the Prohibition Amendment, which had been founded in 1918 and had campaigned

bravely throughout the 'twenties, began to receive increasing
support, particularly from businessmen. The Association's tactics were an exact duplicate of those employed by their arch-
rival the Anti-Saloon League, and their lobbying began to produce results in Washington. Herbert Hoover, the Republican
president who had been elected in 1928 after defeating the 'wet'
candidate Al Smith, came under increasing pressure to reform
the law, and the demands became more urgent after the Wall
Street Crash of 1929.

His administration had started happily for the Anti-Saloon
League with the passage of what was known as the 'Jones Five-
and-Ten Law'. This measure introduced imprisonment for five
years and a fine of $10,000 as a penalty for all prohibition
offenders. It was the last time that the League was able to assert
its dominance over Congress. After the Crash, Congress began
to take account of the feeling in the country and to move steadily
towards reform. The debate on the Jones Law had also served
to highlight a polarization between the parties that was already
common knowledge to the man in the street. The Democrats
were 'wet', and the Republicans were 'dry'. It was a simplifica-
tion, but the public likes simplifications, and with the identification of the Republican Party with the economic disasters of
1929 and 1930, that party's chances in the coming 1932 election didn't look very promising.

In response to the public mood Hoover appointed a commission to study the whole business of prohibition. For eighteen
months it collected evidence and heard witnesses, producing a
monumental report in 1931. The report was a muddle: the
members of the commission could not agree. Two favoured
repeal of the Eighteenth Amendment, five wanted revision and
a government monopoly in liquor, two favoured revision and
further trial of the Amendment, and two supported the *status
quo*. The public and press greeted the report with derision.
Franklin P. Adams's poem, entitled 'The Wickersham Report',
reflects fairly accurately its findings:

> Prohibition is an awful flop.
> We like it.
> It can't stop what it's meant to stop.
> We like it.
> It's left a trail of graft and slime,
> And it don't prohibit worth a dime,
> It's filled our land with vice and crime,
> Nevertheless, we're for it.

In all, however, the report of the Wickersham Committee was a massive defeat for the 'drys'. The commissioners were all supposed to be prohibitionists and yet only two of them were against any revision of the law. Herbert Hoover tried to present the report as a vindication of prohibition, thereby sealing his fate in the coming election.

The Democratic candidate, Franklin D. Roosevelt, said little about prohibition in his campaign, but a great deal about the depression. However, his 'New Deal' included two promises : first, that the Volstead Act would be revised to permit the sale of light wine and beer; second, that a Democratic Congress would vote to place before the people of the several States the issue of ratifying an Act repealing the Eighteenth Amendment. He won the presidency by an overwhelming majority and the Democrats swept to total power in Congress. Prohibition was doomed.

The formalities were carried out on 16 February, 1933, when the Senate passed the Twenty-first Amendment, providing for the repeal of the Eighteenth Amendment, by 63 votes to 23; four days later when the House of Representatives passed the Twenty-first Amendment by 289 to 121; and, finally, on 5 December, 1933, when Utah became the thirty-sixth state to ratify the Twenty-first Amendment. So ended the 'noble experiment'. Prohibition had cost the United States $500 million in futile efforts at enforcement. It had cost the government $5,000 million in revenues. It had cost the lives of thousands of Americans and ruined the health of many other thousands. And it had been directly responsible for the lowering of moral, social and political standards, and for the birth of organized crime.

Its end was celebrated in gin. All over America cocktail shakers were poised, ready for the news of Utah's ratification to be announced on the radio and in the press. Drink was still expensive and hard to come by, but as the news came through every drinker in America made sure that he had a glass of something resembling alcohol in his hand.

Each state could, of course, decide whether to remain 'dry' or go 'wet'. The great majority of the eastern and southern states abolished prohibition immediately but it lingered on in some of the far-western states for a long time to come. In Oklahoma, as we have seen, it lasted until 1959. The saloons came back, but under more moderate and less inflammatory names. They were called taverns, cafés or bars. The old swinging doors, so much a feature of cowboy films (how, after all, can you enter a saloon with both guns blazing when you have to deal with a door handle as well?) were, for some reason, banned. The Anti-Saloon League could console itself that, in this respect at least, it had won a permanent victory.

Europe, too, was suffering a recession, and in its wake came a new danger. In 1933 Hitler gained power in Germany and it soon became clear, at least to those with foresight, that another war was probable before long. As in America, the national mood in Britain was changing; consciously or unconsciously people began to prepare themselves for the storm to come. Drinking habits were inevitably affected, particularly those of the 'leaders of society' who had been the main performers during the Cocktail Age. The cocktail party did not disappear, although by 1937 it was well past its prime. It was replaced by something less frenetic. The huge variety of exotically-named cocktails were ignored and party drinks became standardized around such favourites as the Martini. Sherry, too, became increasingly popular.

Gin, by this point, had reached the zenith of its career: it was numbered among the most civilized drinks in the world, a favourite of businessmen and the members of high society, ladies in particular. Typically, however, it could not entirely shake off the traces of its dissolute past. It was about this time that gin began to acquire the reputation of a do-it-yourself abortifacient. The recommended method was to drink a large amount of gin and then take a very hot bath – as far as one can tell, it was never successful. Some have thought that the name 'mother's ruin' is derived from this activity, but it is undoubtedly much older. The likelihood is that it was coined during the nineteenth century when Victorian matrons drank gin in secret, only to betray themselves by collapsing at a reception or by some similar misadventure, or that it is even older, dating back to the gin-sodden mothers of Hogarth's London.

When war came in 1939 drink was rationed almost immediately. While the brewers combined to produce a uniform (and not very appetizing) wartime beer, the distillers concentrated on supplying the export market in order to help pay for the vast quantities of armaments required. Gin and other spirits were soon in such short supply that they disappeared from shops, bars and public houses. The few precious bottles that publicans could obtain were kept under the counter for regular customers only. Those who have memories of that time will recall only too clearly the ration of one gin-and-tonic a week their local could supply.

Wartime conditions of secrecy and strict control of the media provided a fertile breeding ground for rumours of every possible type. One of the strangest concerned gin. The drink acquired the extraordinary reputation of inducing impotency in men. One can only imagine that this strange theory was the result of a whispering campaign by some rival spirit manufacturer, or even an attempt by the authorities to reduce demand for the little gin that was available. Whatever the case, officers posted abroad who wished to remain faithful to their wives were said to take large quantities of gin in order to lessen the temptations. Of course, this might only have been the excuse they gave to explain their new gin-imbibing habits, for there was plenty of gin to be found once they were abroad.

Those at home with a taste for gin were not so lucky. Substitute gins with weird and terrifying names appeared on the black market. Many of them were reputed to have been distilled on or near the Edgware Road in London, and were known as 'Edgware Road gin'. Some people even went so far as to say that these concoctions were actually *made* from the Edgware Road itself, tarred portions of the public highway being dug up and distilled in secret stills. Certainly, it was a fearful drink, resembling nothing so much as a mixture of methylated spirits and hair oil. When some of the first to try it went literally blind for as long as a week, the demand dropped sharply; and although it had a certain sale in the cheaper Soho nightclubs, most people stuck to the watered-down beer.

To make the best of a worsening situation, the Wine and Spirit Association, with the help of the Ministry of Food under Lord Woolton, devised a quota system. Private customers would be allocated one bottle of gin per month. Sometimes it was difficult to obtain even this modest amount, and the destruction of warehouses at Plymouth was a particular disaster for gin drinkers.

There were, however, 'privileged' people, such as diplomats, naval personnel, army officers on leave from overseas, and, in time, Americans, who seemed somehow always to have a bottle of gin when it was needed. A certain attaché at a foreign embassy in London was once brought before his Ambassador to explain how he managed to drink so many bottles of gin each month. He replied, truthfully, that he gave most of them away to his gin-starved English friends, and defended his action on the grounds that it was an excellent way of 'making friends and influencing people'. Naval officers and servicemen returning from overseas always made a point of bringing some form of spirits – often of a dubious origin, it is true – home with them. But it was the American servicemen, when they came over in their thousands before D-Day, who were the true saviours of many a London party. A familiar sight at the door of a party-giving hostess was the smiling G.I. in his barathea uniform and cocked 'fore-and-aft' cap, holding in one hand a bottle of spirits and in the other a carton of Camel cigarettes.

The wartime drought was responsible for a significant innovation: the bottle party. Each guest would be asked on his invitation to bring a bottle of something to help out the limited supply of drink. The host and hostess would supply the original drinks; somehow they would have secured a bottle or two of gin, which would be mixed with tonic or orange juice (supplied by the Ministry of Food for children and pregnant women). As each guest arrived his bottle would be handed furtively over and hidden to reappear only when the official drinks had run out. No mention was ever made of the fact that new drinks had been brought by the guests themselves; it was not until after the war that the bottle party became an accepted social function and bottles were brought in openly.

The end of the war did not bring an immediate end to the scarcity. Gin remained hard to obtain for some years. At the same time the price rose steadily as Chancellor after Chancellor raised the duty on spirits. Never again would gin be the favourite drink of the poor. It was still drunk by the elderly ladies who frequented the secluded ladies' bars of the old-fashioned Victorian-style public houses, but they – ladies and pubs – gradually disappeared as the all-purpose, lounge-style public house became the vogue.

The new generation, brought up in more egalitarian and monied surroundings, was taking to new-style drinks. Beer, especially bitter and lager, became the basic drink for labourers and office workers alike. Wine increased in popularity as a party drink, and whisky gained ground, taking over to a large extent the cocktail-party role once filled by gin. In more recent times we have seen the rise to popularity of rum and vodka.

By the 1950s most of the more exotic gin-based cocktails had simply disappeared. Even the once popular 'White Lady' vanished like Wilkie Collins' 'Woman in White'. Though barmen can still be seen shaking their cocktail mixers above their heads in the bars of the larger hotels, and some hosts still pour out their guests' drinks through the traditional strainers, it is almost impossible today to obtain some of the once-popular cocktails.

One cocktail that seems to have outlived many others is the rather macabre one known as the Brompton (after the Brompton Hospital in the Fulham Road) or Terminal Cocktail. It is made mainly of gin and diamorphine and is given to patients who are dying as an analgesic.

But, though so many cocktails themselves have passed the terminal stage, they survive in odd places. Recently a national newspaper tried to find out whether a Pink Gin was still obtainable. Although they turned up some deplorable facts as far as the home country was concerned, one barmaid even going so far as to mix half a pint of bitter instead of bitters with the gin, it was found to be flourishing in the remoter parts of the globe.

12

The Old Firms

The practice of taking a fermented mash and distilling it into alcohol goes back, as far as can be ascertained, to the Arabs of the eighth century AD. Certainly the word 'alcohol' is of Arab origin, and an Arab chemist, Anou-Moussah-Djafai-Al-Sofi, gave the first complete description of the process of distillation.

It was left to the more drink-conscious Europeans to use the invention for the purpose of making an intoxicating liquor. At Cordoba, in Spain, a physicist called Albucasis produced, from wine, the first *eau de vie*. In the thirteenth century, Lully, who was born in Mallorca, wrote of *eau de vie* that 'the true water of life comes forth in precious droplets', that is to say, in distillation (the word comes from the Latin *distillare,* to drip). The word 'brandy' is derived from the Dutch *brandewijn,* meaning 'burnt' (i.e. distilled) wine.

Gin, or genever, is therefore a relatively new distilled liquor. The very first gin manufacturing firm in the world opened its doors for business four hundred years ago in 1575 and, remarkably, that firm is still making gin today : the Dutch company, Bols.

The founder was a certain Lucas Bols who intended to set up a plant at Amsterdam, presumably to make aquavit as gin was yet to be invented. The city, however, was extremely fire-conscious and Bols was refused permission to set up his still within the city walls because of the danger from his burners. He chose an alternative site, Plempenpad on the coach road to Haarlem, and there built a little shed ('*t Lootsje* in Dutch), erecting his still in the open air. For cooling, he used the waters of a small stream that ran nearby.

In 1581 Amsterdam changed its fire-hazard laws, so that in 1612, when the city had expanded to take in '*t Lootsje,* the distillery was allowed to remain where it was. By then Jan Jacob Bols, Lucas Bols's son, was in charge of the business. He demolished the original little shed, replacing it with a stone building, but he kept the name '*t Lootsje* in honour of his father. The stream was widened to form a canal called the Rozengracht (Rose Canal) and gardens were laid out along its banks. When the French were occupying Amsterdam they called the area 'Le Jardin', which was distorted by the Dutch into 'Jordaan'. Bols remained there for nearly four centuries, expanding gradually, until 1969 when the company moved to new premises in the small village of Nieuw Vennep outside Amsterdam. But Bols have kept a sampling bar at 106 Rozengracht, a fine gabled house which dates back to 1650 and has associations with Rembrandt and other Dutch painters.

The direct line of the Bols family died out in 1815, and the name of the firm was changed to Erven Lucas Bols (the heirs of Lucas Bols); it is under this name that it is known today. Outside its premises at Nieuw Vennep there is an illuminated sign proclaiming 'Bols Genever Liqueurs', although of course it produces a great many other drinks apart from gin and uses products from all over the world in their manufacture. But to most people, the name Bols stands for the rather special Dutch gin, still referred to as genever or Hollands, which is so different to dry gin. Indeed, if the curious reader wishes for a taste of a gin similar to that which stirred the passions of eighteenth-century Londoners, it is Dutch gin he should ask for.

The other Dutch company famous for its gin is de Kuyper & Zoon of Schiedam, near Rotterdam. Established in 1695 by John de Kuyper, the company is still run by his descendants.

Their chief products are Oude (old) Jenever and Jonge (young) Jenever. The adjectives have nothing to do with ageing but simply refer to the date of the recipe. Recently, a strong demand for a light, white genever has developed, and the Jonge Jenever caters for this taste.

De Kuyper's gins are to be found in square bottles with attractive heart-shaped labels, and were once very popular in Britain; but with supplies completely cut off during World War II, the taste for this type of gin became very restricted. However, there would appear to be a revival of interest in this – to British palates – unusual type of gin. It blends excellently with smoked fish, particularly smoked salmon and smoked eels, and should be drunk neat, as an aperitif, and always chilled.

De Kuyper's also produce an original concoction called Citroenjenever (lemon gin) which is very popular in Holland. Juniper berries are not used at all in its production, but fresh lemon peels, which are distilled in alcohol. A more appropriate English name would probably be lemon vodka. It is used by the Dutch as a flavouring in certain puddings, rather in the way that the British add spirits to Christmas pudding.

In a small booklet entitled *The Mystery of Geneva* by 'John de Kuyper', issued by the firm's publicity department, the author has this to say about the drinking of Dutch gin: 'To the unfamiliar, Hollands Gin has an unfamiliar flavour – a flavour that even the most jaded palate quickly learns to love. Think back on your first glass of beer, or your first whisky and soda. Did you like it? – probably not. But Hollands Gin is one of the simplest flavours that the palate can learn to like. . . .' There are, the reader is told, three ways of drinking it: 'The first is the most usual, and merely calls for a wine glass of sufficient size to hold the desired quantity. Sip it slowly, and let it roll around the tongue, as you might a fine wine – then let it slide gently to its final home within you. Second is for cold days, and calls for a tumbler, and a kettle of hot water. To one part of de Kuyper, add three parts of boiling water, and a slice of lemon to taste – repeating until the kettle is empty. Third is customary in various countries for hot days, when you may add a lump of ice and a splash of ginger ale or soda. But rain or shine, your true Hollander, as we might say, will toss off his merry glass just neat – and very neat it is!'

In Britain, Booth's would appear to be the oldest gin-distilling firm still in existence. Although there is no exact record of when the first Booth turned to making gin, members of the family were engaged in the wine trade as far back as 1569. The Booths had moved down from the north, claiming kinship with the family of that name long settled in Cheshire. One member of the London Booth family was Sir George Booth, who was imprisoned in the Tower of London for his royalist sympathies and, for his pains, was later rewarded with the title of Lord Delamere by Charles II.

Although there is no record of any Booth producing gin during the feverish days of the 1740s and '50s, it is more than likely that some members of the family did so, since all wine merchants of the time were so engaged. There is a record of John Booth paying £10 as a surety for good behaviour on his premises in 1751, relating to the sale of spirits. The first authenti-cated record of the existence of Booth's Distilleries is to be found in the *Directory of Merchants* for 1778. Here Philip Booth and Company, Distillers, are listed as carrying on their business at 55 Turnmill Street in Clerkenwell. Philip was the son of John Booth.

Philip Booth lived for a while in Russell Square, a very fashion-able address, before moving to the village of Crouch End, Hornsey, a convenient four miles from the Clerkenwell distillery. He was evidently a man of some stature, one of the 'brewers, distillers and men in similar departments of trade' whom foreign-ers, according to James Boswell, were 'not a little amazed' to hear being 'held forth as persons of considerable consequence'.

Later, he moved to Mangham's Hill at Waltham Abbey, and then bought another country property in the Hertfordshire village of Stanstead Abbotts. Here the Booths established another branch of the business under the name of William Booth, Philip's eldest son.

After Philip's death in 1818, another of his three sons, Felix, took over control of the firm and expanded it enormously, building a second distillery at Brentford and buying up the Red Lion Brewery at Kew. He added a Scottish branch, and was soon in possession of the largest distillery business in the British Isles. As if this was not enough, he became the first chairman of the Brentford Gas Company, and was responsible for lighting the turnpike road running from Brentford to Kensington. Thus the miraculous gas lamps and the warming spirits that lured the Victorians into the gin palaces were quite possibly the responsibility of the same man.

Felix Booth's interests were not only commercial, but exploratory as well. In 1829 he put up £20,000 for equipping a paddle steamer, the *Victory,* to enable his friend and protégé Captain John Ross to sail to Canada in search of a north-west passage from the Atlantic to the Pacific. The only condition attached to the gift was that Booth's generosity should not be revealed.

The *Victory* left Woolwich Reach on 23 May, 1829. Felix Booth and a young nephew accompanied her as far as Margate. The expedition, alas, was not a success. Reaching Canada the *Victory* was confronted by thick ice and the ship and her crew were forced to spend the first winter in an inlet which Ross called Felix Inlet after his benefactor. By the third winter the ship was so locked in the ice it had to be abandoned, and the fourth was spent in a canvas shelter. By then the expedition had been given up for lost; but in the spring of 1833 they were rescued by Ross's old ship, the *Isabella,* and brought home, landing in triumph at Hull on 18 October, 1833. Although Ross had failed to find the passage, his nephew James Clark Ross had located the true position of the North Magnetic Pole, planting a Union Jack on the spot and celebrating with a toast in Booth's gin. In the meantime Ross had named almost every possible piece of land and sea after his patron. On a map of the area you will find Boothia Peninsular, Felix Harbour, Cape Felix, the Gulf of Boothia and Boothia Isthmus. Even Felix's sisters got a harbour and an island between them.

Ross had not forgotten the 'Sailor King', who was delighted with King William Island. Ross was promptly knighted, and when the identity of his backer was revealed he received a baronetcy, for 'fitting out at his sole cost an expedition to endeavour to discover a North-West Passage'.

Sir Felix Booth, as he thus became, now ranked very high among the merchant princes of the City. He lived in great style at 43 Portland Place and had a Georgian villa in the then rural area of Golders Green. His portrait was painted by Sir Thomas Lawrence and he even became a part of the *Ingoldsby Legends* with the lines:

> Though I own even then I should see no great sin in it
> Were there three drops of Sir Felix's gin in it.

He died at the Royal York Hotel in Brighton in January 1850, while on one of his frequent visits there. He was seventy years of age.

As Sir Felix had never married, the title passed to Williamson Booth, his nephew and another bachelor. On his death it passed to his brother Charles, who was then seventy-one. Charles lived to be ninety and remained a partner in Booth's all his life. Another bachelor – he was said to hate the sight of women – he too left no heir to claim an inheritance that amounted to two million pounds. The title became extinct and the money was divided among his brother Henry's five married daughters.

People have often wondered whether there was any connection between General William Booth, the founder of the Salvation Army, and the distilling family of the same name. General Booth's attitude towards gin was only too forcibly expressed in his book *In Darkest England and the Way Out*: 'The bastard

of a harlot, born in a brothel, suckled on gin, and familiar from
earliest infancy with all the bestialities of debauch, violated
before she is twelve, and driven out into the streets by her
mother a year or two later, what chance is there for such a girl
in this world – I say nothing about the next.'

The belief that General Booth must have been a renegade
member of the gin family was strengthened by the fact that
'Netherfield', Sir Charles Booth's old home at Stanstead Abbotts,
was turned into the Felix Booth Memorial Eventide Home by
the Salvation Army. A marble bust of Sir Felix, unsuitably
attired in Roman gear, was placed in the front hall. There he
gazes down on the 'old soldiers' who live there, many of whom
have presumably never tasted gin in their lives.

The truth, alas, is that there is no family connection between
these two eminent Victorians. Netherfield, with its chairs
stamped with the Booths' family crest of a lion, was presented to
the Salvation Army some years after the death of Sir Charles
Booth by his grandniece, Miss Alice Prior.

Another famous gin, Beefeater London Dry Gin, owes its
origin to the endeavours of one man, James Burrough, who set
up as a distiller in the early part of the nineteenth century.
Born in Devon, Burrough began in business as an apprentice
to an Exeter chemist. While he was being trained he kept a
notebook containing recipes for some very strange-sounding concoctions: *English* champagne, *artificial* asses' milk, and a cure
for all psychiatric disturbances called Sir Henry Halford's Recipe
for Nervous People.

Burrough emigrated to Canada, where he worked as a chemist
for six years. It was on his return to England that he came to
London and set himself up in Chelsea as a distiller of gin and
liqueurs. Chelsea, in the early nineteenth century, was still a
small if fashionable village, linked to the main part of the city
by the King's Road. Burrough's distillery was a little to the
north of the King's Road, in the area of what is now Cale Street.

Here James Burrough distilled many of the exotically-named

10 Gilbey's distillery at Harlow. The distillation unit on the first floor is more than a century old and is still in use.

11 A Victorian distillery.

12 The still-room in Booth's Red Lion Distillery, London.

drinks – among them Lovage, Rosemary Liqueur and Blackberry Brandy – that were so much in fashion in those days. His gin he called Beefeater, as he wanted a traditional name symbolic of London.

After his death the family business was turned into a limited liability company and continued to expand for the rest of the century. By 1908 the Chelsea premises had become too small and a new distillery was built in Lambeth, close to a supply of exceptionally pure water.

The Great War substantially increased the sales of Beefeater Gin, and Burrough's began to develop a very healthy export trade. In 1917 the first shipment of Beefeater to New Orleans was made. Today, the United States is one of the largest customers for Burrough's gin. The Second World War severely inhibited the firm's export drive for a while, but once it was over so determined an effort was made to recapture export markets and develop new ones that by 1963 the company had become the largest gin exporter in the British Isles, accounting for more than half of Britain's total exports of gin. In recognition of this, Burrough's have received the Queen's Award to Industry on more than one occasion. The company has continued to expand, moving into new premises in south London, but somehow the spirit of James Burrough still pervades the distillery and direct descendants of this ambitious chemist are still on the board of the company.

Like acting and politics, the making of drink is often a family tradition. The original founders are usually enterprising and colourful characters, and their descendants tend to follow the family trade. This is particularly true of a gin-producing family like the Gilbeys.

'I remember being told as a child the most extraordinary tales about the Gilbeys and how the firm started,' a member of the family recalled. 'There were, it was said, two brothers in about 1780. One was a miller, the other a coachman. The miller was no good at his job, but behind his mill he operated a still, where he distilled, probably illegally, gin. Whenever his brother, the coachman, passed by, the miller would give him a few bottles of gin to sell at public houses along his route. This gin was so good that soon the coachman was overwhelmed with orders. Hence the origin of the firm.'

There was in fact a Gilbey, Henry Gilbey, who ran a coach on the London to Bishop's Stortford route at that time, but there is no record of a gin-producing brother. Henry's father, Daniel, was a publican, owning three pubs in Stansted, just outside Bishop's Stortford. So perhaps the family legend arose from a confusion of father and son. In all events, Henry Gilbey died, impoverished, in 1842.

An even stranger legend surrounds the development of the business. There was a third brother – in some accounts, a cousin – who ran a public house in the New Forest at the time when the Prince of Wales, or 'Prinny' as he was known, was in the habit of hunting there.

'This Gilbey,' continued my informant, 'had a very attractive wife . . . and nine months after each of the Prince's visits, she would present her husband with a brand new baby. Proof of this royal connection can be found in the fact that, even today, the Gilbeys have the small and beautiful hands and feet of the House of Hanover.

'When Prinny eventually became George IV he was easily persuaded by the two gin-producing brothers to grant them the monopoly in selling wine and spirits in grocers' shops throughout the country, thus assuring the firm of W. & A. Gilbey a permanent market.'

Alas, these romantic tales have very little to do with reality.

When Henry Gilbey, the coachman, died in 1842, he left three sons and three daughters. The eldest son, Henry Parry Gilbey, entered the wine trade. His brothers, Walter and Alfred, went into the army as civilian clerks in the Pay Corps, and were sent to the Crimea. When the war ended in 1856 the two brothers, twenty-six and twenty-four respectively, returned to

London with little money and no qualifications. On the advice of their elder brother they hired cellars on the corner of Oxford Street and Berwick Street and set up in business as W. & A. Gilbey, wine merchants.

The brothers had no capital, but a great deal of luck. The government of the day, in order to encourage wine-growing in the colonies, allowed importers to bring colonial wines into the country at half the duty imposed on French and Spanish wines. The Gilbey brothers concentrated on South Africa and offered Cape port and sherry at twenty shillings a dozen, and brandy at thirty shillings a dozen. At this stage there was no talk of gin.

The Cape wines proved so popular that within a few months the new firm had 20,000 customers on its books. In 1860, when Gladstone reduced the duty on French wine, the Gilbey brothers were ready to take advantage of the new demand for cheap wines: 'Gladstone claret', as it was known, made their fortune.

The business continued to prosper and expand throughout the remainder of the nineteenth century, but very little of this expansion was due to sales of gin. Even by 1914, when the firm's premises at Camden Town covered twenty acres and the bottling stores could hold 800,000 gallons, gin was only a small part of the business. It was the First World War that brought a boost to Gilbey's gin trade. Smaller firms went under as wartime restrictions were introduced, but Gilbey's were able to maintain a steady supply of gin by rectifying their Cape spirit supplies. And when the war ended, the new craze for cocktails gave great impetus to the sales of Gilbey's gin.

Subsidiary gin-producing firms were established in Australia and Canada; and in the United States after the repeal of prohibition in 1933. Not that Gilbey's gin was unknown to Americans during the 'dry' years of the 'twenties. On the contrary, unobtrusive American gentlemen made frequent visits to Gilbey's head office in London, carrying huge amounts of cash and placing orders for gallons of Gilbey's London Gin to be wrapped in hessian bags and dispatched to Hamburg or

Antwerp. There the bootleggers took over and the gin, by way of Canada, Nassau or Newfoundland, found its way into the speakeasies of America.

Such was the popularity of the gin that got past the US customs that the moonshiners began to label their own dubious products 'Gilbey's'. The firm received so many requests for the identification of genuine labels that it was forced to set up a special identification office. The watermark in the paper always gave the vital clue.

To make things easier, Gilbey's produced a special bottle – square, sand-blasted on three sides, with the label printed on both sides and visible through the one clear side – which was very difficult and costly to imitate. This bottle was used until recently for Gilbey's USA gin.

Most romantically situated of all gin manufacturers are Coates & Company, the makers of Plymouth gin. Their head-quarters are in the old Black Friars Monastery in Plymouth. Founded in 1425, the monastery became a debtors' prison after Henry VIII's Dissolution of the Monasteries in 1536; its fine-beamed refectory was the Town Meeting Place. It was here, in 1620, that the Pilgrim Fathers were reputed to have had their final meeting before setting sail in the *Mayflower* for America. It was here too that the first Huguenots, fleeing from persecution in France, gathered on their arrival in England.

Just over a hundred years later, in 1793, the monastery was acquired by Coates. Although badly damaged during the war the refectory hall was restored in 1961 and is still part of the firm's premises.

Plymouth gin is not seen so often these days, but it remains the favourite of the Royal Navy, who insist that a proper pink gin cannot be made with anything else.

Finally, there is the immensely popular Gordon's Gin. At one time Gordon's employed elegant young men to walk into bars and public houses and ask simply for a gin-and-tonic; if the barman did not reach automatically for the square, green

Gordon's bottle, he would be gently reminded that the word 'gin' was synonymous with 'Gordon's'.

A modern distillery looks somewhat like the engine room of a large liner. There is the same cleanliness, the iron walks, the steel steps rising through three floors, the huge vats resembling boilers, the burnished pipes and the men in white coats carefully watching gauges.

The juniper berries usually come from Morocco; they are dehydrated black berries, and cost at least £800 a ton. Distillers buy them in sacks and keep a two-or three-year stock in hand. Other ingredients include coriander, a pale berry which also comes from North Africa, and small quantities of angelica, orris-root and cassia bark.

The rectifying of the sugar cane or grain alcohol takes place in huge stills weighing between $5\frac{1}{2}$ and $8\frac{1}{2}$ tons. Up until the war, they were made of hand-beaten copper. Now, they are made by machinery. The heating is usually done by coil heaters. The vapour rises to the coolers and then flows as liquid down to the storage tanks on the ground floor. Checks are made at various stages.

An important part of a modern distillery is the export area. Here the gin goes out in steel barrels (which are returnable) to all parts of the world. Tests are taken that the gin is of exactly the right strengths for different countries. National strengths vary considerably, and almost all are stronger than the gin destined for the home market. One of the strongest gins is that sent to Argentina.

Every large distillery today has an efficient laboratory. Here samples of gins are tested to see that they are the correct strengths and purity. Also tested in the laboratories are the extra ingredients such as coriander. The amount of oil that can be extracted from the coriander or juniper berries from different areas can be determined in the laboratory, and this will help the firm to decide where to buy its next supplies. Gin, like whisky, is now international. More of it is drunk overseas than in its country of origin, a development that would have surprised William III had he known this would happen when he gave gin the go-ahead two and a half centuries ago.

13

'When I'm So Dispoged'

Although Alexander Pope had intervened, during the great struggle between gin and beer in the eighteenth century, to warn that :

> Vice thus abused, demands a nation's care,
> This calls the church to deprecate our sin,
> And hurls the thunder of our laws on gin.

it was not until the next century that a great author was to do gin full justice in his work. That author was Charles Dickens.

In his first book, *Sketches by Boz* (1836) he gave the marvellous description of a gin palace which we have already reproduced in an earlier chapter. In his second book, *The Pickwick Papers,* he returned to the subject of gin, but this time he focused his satirical eye on those who were 'partial to a drop'. In 'The Story of the Goblins who Stole a Sexton', Gabriel Grub, the bad-tempered sexton, goes out on Christmas Even to dig a grave and have a quiet drink. In the graveyard he meets a goblin :

> 'What man wanders among graves and churchyards on such a night as this?' cried the goblin.
> 'Gabriel Grub! Gabriel Grub!' screamed a wild chorus of voices that seemed to fill the churchyard. Gabriel looked

fearfully around – nothing was to be seen.

'What have you got in that bottle?' said the goblin.

'Hollands, sir', replied the sexton, trembling more than ever, for he had bought it from the smugglers, and he thought that perhaps his questioner might be in the excise department of the goblins.

The bad-tempered sexton, who has cuffed a boy on the way to the graveyard, is shown, rather as Scrooge is in *A Christmas Carol,* scenes from different lives and is converted to a happier frame of mind. He leaves his village, only to return ten years later 'a ragged, contented, rheumatic old man', and when he tells of his fantastic meeting with the goblins his listeners 'shrugged their shoulders, touched their foreheads, and murmured something about Gabriel Grub having drunk all the Hollands. . . .'

Hollands is also mentioned earlier on in *The Pickwick Papers,* when Sam Weller first meets Job Trotter at the Angel at Bury St. Edmunds, and asks:

'Will you take a drop o'somethin' this mornin', Mr. Trotter?'

Mr. Trotter acquiesced in this agreeable proposal: and having deposited his book in his coat-pocket, accompanied Mr. Weller to the Tap, where they were soon occupied in discussing an exhilarating compound, formed by mixing together, in a pewter vessel, certain quantities of British Hollands, and the fragrant essence of the clove.

It was not only the gin drinkers who caught Dickens's eye. Their opponents, the temperance reformers, were perfect material for him. In *The Pickwick Papers* Sam Weller and his father, who is horrified at the amount of tea being drunk, find themselves at a meeting of the Brick Lane Branch of the United Grand Junction Ebenezer Temperance Association. The com-

mittee's secretary has the 'unspeakable pleasure' of reporting
recent cases of conversion to temperance, one of whom, H.
Walker, a tailor :

> 'says he is not certain whether he did not twice a week, for
> twenty years, taste "dog's nose" which your committee find
> upon inquiry, to be compounded of warm porter, moist
> sugar, gin, and nutmeg (a groan, and "So it is!" from an
> elderly female).'

Another convert is Thomas Burton, purveyor of cat's meat to
the Lord Mayor and Sheriffs, who, the secretary reports :

> 'Has a wooden leg; finds a wooden leg expensive, going over
> the stones; used to wear second-hand wooden legs, and drink
> a glass of hot gin and water regularly every night – sometimes
> two (deep sighs). Found the second-hand wooden legs split
> and rot very quickly; is firmly persuaded that their constitu-
> tion was undermined by gin and water (prolonged cheering).
> Buys new wooden legs now, and drinks nothing but water
> and weak tea. The new legs last twice as long as the others
> used to do, and he attributes this solely to his temperance
> habits (triumphant cheers).'

Another scene, later in the book, shows that gaolers and turnkeys in Dickens's time were still not averse to supplying their
charges with gin – at a price. Mr Pickwick has been confined
in the debtors' prison, The Fleet, and is invited by Job Trotter
to a whistling shop :

> 'What do you mean?' was Mr. Pickwick's counter enquiry.
> 'A vistlin' shop, sir', interposed Mr. Weller.
> 'What is that, Sam? A bird-fancier's?' inquired Mr.
> Pickwick.
> 'Bless your heart, no, sir', replied Job, 'a whistling shop,

sir, is where they sell spirits'. Mr. Job Trotter briefly explained here, that all persons, being prohibited under heavy penalties from conveying spirits into debtors' prisons, and such commodities being highly prized by the ladies and gentlemen confined therein, it had occurred to some speculative turnkey to connive, for certain lucrative consideration at two or three prisoners retailing the favourite article of gin, for their own profit and advantage.

'This plan, you see sir, has been gradually introduced into all prisons for debt', said Mr. Trotter.

'And it has this wery great advantage', said Sam, 'that the turnkeys takes wery good care to seize hold o' ev'ry body but them as pays 'em, that attempts the williany, and wen it gets in the papers they're applauded for their wigilance; so it cuts two ways – frightens other people from the trade, and elewates their own characters'.

Dickens was always fond of revealing indirectly the foibles of his characters. When, in *Oliver Twist,* Mr Bumble, the Beadle, visits Mrs Mann to whom the poor orphan Oliver has been farmed out, the following conversation takes place :

'Now don't be offended at what I am going to say', observed Mrs. Mann, with captivating sweetness. 'You've had a long walk, you know or I wouldn't mention it. Now will you take a little drop of somethink, Mr. Bumble?'

'Not a drop. Not a drop', said Mr. Bumble, waving his right hand in a dignified, but placid manner.

'I think you will', said Mrs. Mann, who had noticed the tone of the refusal, and the gesture that had accompanied it. 'Just a leetle drop, with a little cold water, and a lump of sugar'.

Mr. Bumble coughed.

'Now, just a leetle drop', said Mrs. Mann persuasively.

'What is it,' enquired the beadle.

'Why, it's what I'm obliged to keep a little of in the house, to put into the blessed infants' Daffy, when they aint well, Mr. Bumble', replied Mrs. Mann as she opened a corner cupboard, and took down a bottle and glass. 'It's gin. I'll not deceive you, Mr. B. It's gin'.

Gin was then – *Oliver Twist* was published in 1837-8 – still very much the drink of the poor, the disreputable and the criminal. When the Artful Dodger first brings Oliver to Fagin, the latter 'mixed him a glass of hot gin and water : telling him he must drink it off directly, because another gentleman wanted the tumbler'.

When Bill Sikes, the burglar, has a fever, he takes 'hot water with his gin to render it less inflammatory'. Nancy gets drunk to forget her wretchedness and the fact that she is a member of Fagin's gang. When the latter visits her, searching for Oliver, he finds her drunk, while 'a wholesale perfume of Geneva' fills the room.

Though gin is, throughout the book, cast as a depraving drink – the good Mr Brownlow and his friend Mr Grimwig would have a decanter on their table – it is not the motivating force of any of the characters. Mr Bumble, Sikes and Nancy all have definite personalities. Their drinking is just a passing expression of their failings.

It was not until *Martin Chuzzlewit* was published in 1843-4 that the first full gin-character appears in fiction. She is Sairey Gamp, a nurse and midwife who 'lodged at a bird-fancier's, next door but one to the celebrated mutton-pie shop, and directly opposite to the original cat's-meat warehouse. . . .'

Mrs Gamp appears in the book at the time when Mr Pecksniff, at Jonas Chuzzlewit's request, is seeking a nurse to sit with the body of old Anthony Chuzzlewit. Her partiality to spirits is made plain from the very start :

The face of Mrs. Gamp – the nose in particular – was somewhat red and swollen, and it was difficult to enjoy her society without becoming conscious of a smell of spirits.

Mrs Gamp defends her need for stimulants, and at the same time underlines the fact that she drinks very little, by quoting a conversation with her non-existent friend, Mrs Harris :

' "Mrs. Harris", I says, at the very last as ever I acted in, which it was but a young person, "Mrs. Harris", I says, "leave the bottle on the chimney piece, and don't ask me to take none, but let me put my lips to it when I am so dispoged, and then I will do what I'm engaged to do, according to the best of my ability". "Mrs. Gamp", she says, in answer, "if ever there was a sober creetur to be got at eighteen pence a day for working people, and three and six for gentlefolk – night watching", said Mrs. Gamp, with emphasis, "being a extra charge – you are that inwallable person".'

Oddly enough, although it is assumed that the bottle on the chimney piece contains gin, no actual mention is made of the name of the drink; Dickens, like Mrs Gamp, maintains a discreet silence. Indeed, it is only when, on another occasion, she is ordering her supper from an assistant chambermaid that the word is mentioned at all :

'And whatever you do, young woman, don't bring more than a shilling's-worth of gin and warm water when I rings the bell a second time; for that is always my allowance, and I never takes a drop beyond !'

Which, considering one could get nicely tipsy on threepence-worth of gin at that time, is not ungenerous.

At the conclusion of the famous tea party between Mrs Gamp and her friend and colleague, Betsey Prig, Mrs Gamp takes

Mrs Gamp.
Drawing by H. K. Browne

down the teapot that she always keeps on the chimney piece, and although neither she nor the author are indelicate enough to say so, it is quite obvious that the colourless spirit poured into the waiting glasses is gin. There are still in existence Victorian teapots of the type Sairey Gamp might have used. They have a special chamber inside the main one, where the necessary spirits can be secreted.

'Betsey', said Mrs. Gamp, filling her own glass, and passing the teapot, 'I will now propoge a toast. My frequent pardner,

Betsey Prig!'

'Which, altering the name to Sairah Gamp; I drink', said
Mrs. Prig, 'with love and tenderness'.

But, despite this display of affection, the two ladies are not
at all in harmony, and with 'every application of the teapot'
the dispute between them is increased, until :

. . . Mrs. Prig, without any abatement of her offensive
manner, again counterfeited abstraction of mind, and
stretched out her hand to the teapot. It was more than Mrs.
Gamp could bear. She stopped the hand of Mrs. Prig with
her own, and said, with great feeling :

'No, Betsey! Drink fair, wotever you do!'

Mrs. Prig, thus baffled, threw herself back in her chair,
and closing the same eye more emphatically, and folding her
arms tighter, suffered her head to roll slowly from side to side,
while she surveyed her friend, with a contemptuous smile.

Mrs. Gamp resumed :

'Mrs. Harris, Betsey – '

'Bother Mrs. Harris!' said Betsey Prig.

Mrs. Gamp looked at her with amazement, incredulity, and
indignation; when Mrs. Prig, shutting her eye still closer, and
folding her arms still tighter, uttered these memorable and
tremendous words :

'I don't believe there's no sich a person!'

Even when Paul Sweedlepipe, the bird-fancier, John West-
lock, Tom Pinch's friend, and Martin Chuzzlewit come to her
assistance after the treacherous Mrs Prig has left, the real
contents of the troublesome teapot are still not fully revealed :

Mrs. Gamp shed more tears, shook her head and feebly
pronounced Mrs. Harris's name.

'Have a little – '. John was at a loss what to call it.

'Tea', suggested Martin.

'It ain't tea', said Mrs. Gamp.

'Physic of some sort, I suppose', cried John. 'Have a little'.

Mrs Gamp's exit from the pages of Dicken's novel is as satisfactory as her first appearance. After Jonas Chuzzlewit and Mr Pecksniff have been unmasked, old Martin Chuzzlewit suggests mildly enough that she might drink rather less, be more honest and give more sympathy to her patients :

Mrs. Gamp clasped her hands, turned up her eyes until they were quite invisible, threw back her bonnet for the admission of fresh air to her heated brow; and in the act of saying faintly – 'Less liquor! – Sairey Gamp – Bottle on the chimney-piece, and let me put my lips to it, when I'm so dispoged!' – fell into one of the walking swoons; in which pitiable state she was conducted forth by Mr. Sweedlepipe. . . .

Even Dickens's minor references to gin are memorable. There's something rather charming about the way the disreputable Silas Wegg in *Our Mutual Friend* confides to Mr Boffin, who has engaged him to read the 'Decline-and-Fall-Off-The-Rooshan-Empire' that 'I generally do it on gin and water.'

Gin occurs in the works of other Victorian writers, though not to the same degree. Thus, in *Tom Brown's Schooldays*, while most of the boys drink beer, Flashman has to be different and have Gin Punch; and in *The History of Pendennis* Thackeray's hero finds that Gin-twist has 'no charms'. In the twentieth century only in the works of Evelyn Waugh has the new, sophisticated gin drinker received proper consideration. Waugh, in his early novels, surveyed the world of the Bright Young Things and they, of course, drank cocktails.

It is a cocktail of sorts that Paul Pennyfeather offers Captain Grimes and Mr Prendergast in *Decline and Fall*, when he invites them out to dinner at the Hotel Metropole, Cwmpryddyg. It has this effect on Mr Prendergast :

'I believe it's their keys,' said Mr Prendergast suddenly. It was the first time he had spoken. For twenty minutes he had been sitting very upright in his gilt chair and very alert, his eyes unusually bright, darting this way and that in his eagerness to miss nothing of the gay scene about him.

'What's their keys, Prendy?'

'Why, the things they get given at the counter. I thought for a long time it was money.'

In poetry too, gin's appearance has usually been of a rather slight and somewhat sardonic nature. When the drink does appear it is more often than not a rhyme for 'sin'. Perhaps no one carried off this rather limited rhyme more successfully than A. P. Herbert with his poignant plea :

> Don't tell my mother I'm living in sin,
>   Don't let the old folks know.
> Don't tell my twin that I breakfast on gin.
>   He'd never survive the blow.

Other examples are this anonymous little ditty, popular with partygoers a few years ago :

> I'm tired of gin,
> I'm tired of sin,
> And after last night,
> Oh boy, am I tired.

this complaint from a frustrated American during the prohibition period :

> Forty miles from whisky,
>   And sixty miles from gin,
> I'm leaving this damn country,
>   For to live a life of sin.

and finally, this verse by John Masefield, the late Poet Laureate :

> Meanwhile, my friend, would be no sin
> To mix more water in your gin.
> We're neither saints nor Philip Sidneys
> But mortal men with mortal kidneys.

The same rhyme scheme even appears in Edward Fitzgerald's celebrated translation of *The Rubaiyat of Omar Khayyam* :

> O thou who didst with Pitfall and with Gin,
> Beset the road I was to wander in,
> Thou wilt not with Predestination round,
> Enmesh me, and impute my Fall to sin.

Alas, however, for those of us who enjoy the mental picture of the old Persian sipping dry Martinis beneath his famous tree, the gin here is a snare or trap and not the potent spirit.

A. P. Herbert, in another poem, does manage to avoid rhyming 'gin' with 'sin'. The result is charming, and is possessed of great wisdom :

> Well, if it isn't gin,
> Was meant to do us in,
> The chances are it's lemonade or dates.

The last word, however, must go to Auguste Barbier, the nineteenth-century French poet. Even those whose French is rudimentary will appreciate these lines :

Du gin, du gin! – à plein verre, garçon!
Dans ses flots d'or, cette rude boisson
Roule le ciel et l'oublie de soi-même.

In the theatre, gin has a longer and more varied history. From 'Jack Juniper's' *Deposing and Death of Queen Gin,* temperance plays, and the music hall, to the drawing-room comedies of the Cocktail Age and T. S. Eliot's *The Cocktail Party,* gin has often taken a starring role. In the temperance plays, gin is of course the villain. The usual theme is a gin-drinking mother bringing ruin upon her family. In the midst of these tedious and sanctimonious tracts, the occasional line does catch the eye and bring an unintended smile to the lips of the contemporary reader. One unrecorded playwright has left us the memorable line : 'Out, wretched woman – and take your bottle with you.'

In the music hall gin was one of the standard jokes, as much a 'must' as the red-nosed comic staggering in from the wings. (Imitating a drunk is, incidentally, supposed to be one of the easiest tricks to learn. But it requires the magic touch of a Jack Train, in the old ITMA shows, with his 'I-don't-mind-if-I-do' approach to the slightest suggestion of a drink, to reach perfection.) There are many references to gin in the old music hall songs and ballads; most are of an admonitory nature and addressed to the female members of the audience, such as this appeal to Mrs Moore :

Too many double gins give the ladies double chins,
So don't have any more, Mrs Moore.

When gin achieved respectability, its portrayal on the stage naturally changed. However, even in the 1930s, it retained a trace of wickedness, as in the 'anthem' of the debutantes in Noel Coward's *Words and Music* :

For Gin, in cruel
Sober Truth,
Supplies the Fuel
For Flaming Youth.

It remained for T. S. Eliot to elevate the drawing-room comedy, and thus gin itself, into the realms of high art. In *The Cocktail Party* gin assumes an almost religious significance:

EDWARD : Don't go yet, Don't go yet.
We'll finish the cocktails.
Or would you rather have whisky?
UNIDENTIFIED GUEST : Gin.
EDWARD : Anything in it?
UNIDENTIFIED GUEST : A drop of water.

A little later, the strange, unidentified guest asks for another gin and water. This time he adds: 'Let me prepare it for you, if I may. . . . Strong . . . but sip it slowly . . . and drink it sitting down.'

14

Gin Marches On

The story of gin has been partly the story of the drink's opponents, that persistent band of characters who have never completely given up hope of ridding this planet of gin and similar intoxicating liquors for ever. The campaign has lost some of its fervour and most of its support, but a few dedicated tee-totallers and prohibitionists are carrying on the tradition of Joseph Livesey and Carry Nation, sharing a little of the former's optimism and the latter's eccentricity. In the 1972 American presidential election, as in all the elections before it, the Pro-hibition Party put up candidates for the offices of President and Vice-President; between them they polled precisely 13,444 votes. It seems that drink is no longer the issue it once was.

In Britain, the temperance reformers are equally unsuccessful, often having abandoned the drink issue to attack other 'evils' of the 'permissive society'. First it was the corrupting effect of cinema-going, now it is violence, immorality, drugs and promiscuity. In 1964 the General Secretary of the Band of Hope warned that with 'juvenile delinquency . . . promiscuity and drug taking . . . rapidly undermining the nation . . . the collapse of our civilisation' was an imminent possibility. As Norman Longmate comments sadly in the closing chapter of *The Water-drinkers*: 'The temperance movement today has in fact little in common with its past. Its progressive love of humanity has degenerated into reactionary opposition to "softness", its old comradeship has withered into fraternal distrust, its desire to improve the quality of life has congealed into a joyless puritanism.'

In the 'fifties and 'sixties gin rather lost its grip on the mass of the people. It became unpopular with the young. It was too expensive. It could not compete with either the much cheaper beer or with wine. It was, with all spirits, a favoured target of a Chancellor seeking more funds. It became an 'establishment' drink.

Oddly enough, while British gin lost popularity in its country of origin, it gained abroad. With gin no longer looked upon as a 'Limey' drink, the names of British gin manufacturers could be seen on the hoardings of New York advertising sites. Subsidiary companies were set up in a number of places, and great care was taken in the preparation of the gin destined for export. Gilbey's, for example, constructed a special sampling room where gins of the favourites tastes and strengths for nations all over the world were kept. Export gin is generally stronger than the gin distilled for the home market, as travellers returning with duty-free bottles will testify. Different labels are often used. Gordon's export bottles have a brightly-coloured label with pictures of juniper berries on it, which its home-market counterpart lacks.

As the drinking of gin increased abroad, so new drinking habits were re-imported to Europe. Holland's gin has increased in world popularity, particularly in the colder and harder parts of the globe. It is a strengthener, returning to its original function of keeping out the cold mists of the Dutch polders. English gin, and particularly London dry gin, has become the basis of smart drinks in the newer, refurbished public houses. Once again the young are returning to the habit of gin drinking, not the frenetic Bright Young Things of the 'twenties, but the cool, calculating young executives of the 'seventies. There is even a chance that the recent wave of nostalgia for the 'twenties and 'thirties might bring about the return of the cocktail.

Gin has also regained a measure of the medical recognition it had when it first set out on its journey. It is good for gout, rheumatism and bladder and kidney complaints. Diabetics can drink gin because of its low carbohydrate content, and those suffering with gall-stones are often put on a diet of gin and water. Finally, a little gin at childbirth is said to ease the pains of labour. It has gone full circle, from mother's ruin to mother's help.

It is, perhaps, on this cheering note that this book may close. Gin, the youngest of the classic alcoholic drinks, has somehow in its relatively short career been billed in the most diverse of roles : doctor, villain, murderer, fop and dandy. Beginning just over four hundred years ago as an obscure medicine, little known outside the Low Countries, it took nearly one hundred and fifty years, and a political move on the part of William III, to turn it into the scourge of a country. Its reputation as a debaucher and a killer clung on for a further one hundred and fifty years. Only now has gin received the international recognition and achieved the respectability it has been seeking for so long.

BIBLIOGRAPHY

Bickerdyke, John, *The Curiosities of Ale and Beer* (1889), Spring Books, 1965.

Bradstreet, Dudley, *The Life and Uncommon Adventures of Capt. Dudley Bradstreet*, 1754.

Catlin, George E. G., *Liquor Control*, Thornton Butterworth, 1931.

Cooper, A., *The Complete Distiller*, J. Hamilton, 1797.

Doxat, John, *Booth's Handbook of Cocktails and Mixed Drinks*, Pan Books, 1966.

———, *Drinks and Drinking*, Ward Lock, 1971.

Fisher, Irving, *Prohibition at its Worst*, Macmillan, 1926.

French, Richard Valpy, *Nineteen Centuries of Drink in England*, Longmans Green, 1884.

George, M. Dorothy, *London Life in the 18th Century*, Kegan Paul, Trench and Trubner, 1925.

Harrison, Brian, *Drink and the Victorians*, Faber & Faber, 1971.

Kinross, Lord, *The Kindred Spirit: A History of Gin and the House of Booth*, Newman Neame, 1959.

Longmate, Norman, *The Waterdrinkers*, Hamish Hamilton, 1968.

Marrison, L. W., *Wines and Spirits*, Penguin, 1957.

Nation, Carry, *The Use and Need of the Life of Carry A. Nation*, Topeka, 1908.

'Robert', *Cocktails : How to Mix Them*, Herbert Jenkins, n.d.

Rudé, George, *Hanoverian London*, Secker & Warburg, 1971.

Sinclair, Andrew, *Prohibition*, Faber & Faber, 1962.

Waugh, Alec, *Merchants of Wine: Being a Centenary Account of the Fortunes of the House of Gilbey*, Cassell, 1957.

Whipple, Sidney B., *Noble Experiment*, Methuen, 1934.

INDEX

149